Ana

Analysing Adolescence

Paul van Heeswyk

sheldon PRESS

First published in Great Britain in 1997 by
Sheldon Press, SPCK, Marylebone Road, London NW1 4DU

The author and publisher would like to thank the following for permission to use material in this book:
Faber and Faber Ltd ('The Love Song of J. Alfred Prufrock', in *Collected Poems* 1909–1962, T. S. Eliot, 1963).
Faber and Faber Ltd ('This be the Verse', in *High Windows*, Philip Larkin, 1974).
Faber and Faber Ltd ('The Buddha of Suburbia', Hanif Kureishi, 1990).
Dwarf Music ('Highway 61 Revisited, Bob Dylan).

British Library Cataloguing-in-Publication Data
A catalogue record for this book is available from the British Library

ISBN 0–85969–722–3

Photoset by Deltatype Ltd, Birkenhead, Merseyside
Printed in Great Britain by
Biddles Ltd, Guildford and King's Lynn

Contents

Acknowledgements

I am inspired by and have been changed by the following authors and their books: Ernest Becker, Barbara Dockar Drysdale, Judith Ennew, Paul Goodman, Ivan Illich, James Kincaid, Joel Kovel, Adam Phillips, Janice Raymond.

I would like to thank the following people for their contributions and support: Jo' Carritt, Alex Coren, Dr Christopher Dare, Robert Fleming, Wallace Hamilton, Lia Kahn, Celia Lines, Anna Motz, Niki Parker, Kier Simmons, Vera Vasarhelyi and Peter Wilson, Director of Young Minds. I have greatly appreciated the literary and editing talents of Victoria Davenport.

I have gained an immense amount from conversations with John Whitwell, Pat Hancock, Chris Knight, Kay Malko, Peter Millar and Patrick Tomlinson. Ann Whitwell wrote a beautiful children's story, and Steve Lund taught me something that I have used in this book. I am proud to have worked with all of you, staff and boys, at the Cotswold Community, and with you, Ian Warburton.

Nechamah Inbar Bonanos was alongside me at all stages as teacher and friend. Her intelligent reading, insights and special company made the writing of this book better and much more fun. Dorann van Heeswijk rescued the project at critical times. Her unique ideas moved me on and gave me new ways of seeing.

I am grateful to William Donovan, Junior Hibbert, David Maggs, Micheline Mason, Ans Sarianamual and Kier Simmons for sharing their thoughts and stories with me.

Anna and Joseph van Heeswijk, and my friends Michael and Daphne Bonanos; Gaika, Kibwe and Zenna Tavares and Hernan Morilla, always raise my spirits and awareness to the highest levels.

I love my mother's lively mind and her generous enjoyment of all those people she meets. I am deeply saddened that Anton van Heeswijk's laughter of pleasure and gentle teasing will not greet the publication of this book.

There will be time, there will be time
To prepare a face to meet the faces that you meet . . .
T.S. Eliot

For Adam Phillips. Twenty years of friendship – laughing and learning.

Introduction

Kiss Me Razumikhin

Young people are a minority, and a minority, as Ibsen points out, is always right. There is, it is true, an age of majority when they can join us, but for the most part we refer to young people as minors – especially when what is at issue is indulgence or participation in those pleasures or activities that we feel we need to restrict to ourselves, and when there exists a certain doubt as to their value: sex; the consumption of recreational drugs like alcohol and tobacco; work.

'A minority exists', writes Paul Goodman, (1969) 'because of a psychic boundary that makes a real or fancied distinction relevant and the anxious clustering and self-identification of the "majority" to keep on the right side.' All minorities carry repudiated parts of ourselves; it is what we repress in ourselves and project into such groups that creates them as a minority in the first place and sustains and perpetuates them as this. The reason any minority is always right, therefore, is that it is asking for what we want, while being saddled, often, with what we do not. Clearly it is moral and psychological wisdom for the majority to own up and take back.

This is another young man's book, and I struggle with a paradox that comically betrays me. Whenever I read or listen to a story, I notice that I cannot concentrate fully on the action or plot until I have been told the ages of the characters involved. Yet I can never remember my own age, nor the ages of my friends and family; nor even those of the children and young people who I meet in the course of my work. This can be awkward and embarrassing sometimes, as you would imagine. Do I need to worry?

To begin my own story, I sought a phrase that I thought I remembered from Freud which captured, I felt, essential aspects of the labels and pressure that we put on our young people.

When I finally managed to track down the quote I discovered that my memory was better. On the way, however, I stumbled on the following:

> The savage [sic] Timmes of Sierra Leone who elect their king, reserve to themselves the right of beating him on the eve of his coronation; and they avail themselves of this constitutional privilege with such hearty goodwill that sometimes the unhappy monarch does not survive his elevation to the throne (Freud, 1913; Frazier 1911).

We never live wholly in present time, said the philosopher Regis Debray (1968). History appears on the stage, wearing the mask of the previous scene. Or to be more specific, our media attacks on our betters are not, as we thought, news. But tradition or not, we do need to think more about these beatings we mete out to the royals in the Palaces of Buckingham and Westminster. It is after all our lives they are leading. And as we think of our young with those other attitudes of solicitude and deference, we know that we dream also, in other guise, of hostility and neglect.

These royals are family all right, and what is more, the one we all believe ourselves to have been born into. They must then be allowed every freedom, privilege and indulgence, just as we were, or should have been. We prescribe their excess, that is the phrase, and then punish them for it. We also do this to our youth.

The word 'adolescence' comes from the Latin. There is, however, some dispute among historians about when adolescence was first thought in the West to be a definite developmental stage of life. Philipe Aries (1962) thought it unlikely, for example, that adolescence was recognized before the end of the nineteenth century. Lawrence Stone (1977), however, quotes from the autobiography, written in 1576, of the Elizabethan musician Thomas Wythorne: 'After the age of childhood (0–15) beginneth the age named adolescency, which continueth until twenty and five'.

What is clearly beyond doubt is that adults have been complaining about young people since the beginning of recorded history. Probably one of the earliest and best-known examples is that of Hesiod, who declared in the eighth century BC:

> I see no hope for the future of our people if they are dependent on the frivolous youth of today, for certainly all youth are reckless beyond words . . . When I was a boy, we were taught to be discreet and respectful of elders, but the present youth are exceedingly wise and impatient of restraint.

The shepherd in *The Winter's Tale* continues the theme, but Shakespeare fleshes it out a little to make certain we realize what his problems are:

> I would there were no age between ten and three-and-twenty, or that youth would sleep out the rest; for there is nothing in the between but getting wenches with child, wronging the ancientry, stealing, fighting.

Disraeli is more openly in conflict. He once described youth as 'a blunder' but also, on another occasion, said, 'Almost everything that is great has been done by youth.'

It seems that for adults adolescence has always been seen as a time of unpredictable and selfish behaviour, moodiness, over-sensitivity and touchiness. It is also seen as a special period of hope, possibility and freedom; a phase of high energy, excitement and creativity. Even these latter views are often tempered, however, by cynicism and regret: 'youth is wasted on the young'.

Typically views held by adults in regard to adolescents are, to say the least, ambivalent. We see them as vulnerable victims, or as young sadists who inflict terrible damage on others; we fear them as posing grave danger to our cars, property, jobs, morals and way of life, or fear for them as an endangered species requiring special protection; we envy their freedom and hopefulness, or cling to them as the only hope for ourselves and the planet; we curse and constrain their wild impulsivity, or seek to facilitate and encourage their escape from the repressive convention that constrains the school-children that they were, and the adults they will become.

Developmental tasks

The tradition in psychoanalytic accounts of adolescence is to emphasize a teleology of developmental tasks. Adolescence begins with biology and ends with psychology. It is kick-started by puberty and cruises slowly to a halt at adult identity, the point at which the petrol is getting low and we need to think about saving it for the long, straight road ahead. The developmental tasks can be summarized in this way:

- The moving away from the close and familiar security of home and school to the wider variety of people and ideas in the world at large.
- Ownership of the body, which previously was held under a kind of leasing arrangement with the parents; this will involve integrating into the body image the newly awakened sexual feelings and fantasies, as well as rapid changes in size and strength.
- The attainment of personal autonomy and becoming a separate person; this is usually taken to mean the establishment of a confidence in and a sense of responsibility for one's beliefs and actions.
- The achievement of intimacy with others based on secure personal boundaries and a fixed sexual identity.
- Adaptation to the adult world of work and care of the young, with the twin values of the identification and pursuit of personal and career goals, and commitment to agreements entered into and tasks undertaken.

In order to be certain that we do have a proper and worthy subject to study and that we have important things to say about it, we divide adolescence, in the best Judaeo-Christian traditions of the Haggadah and the Trinity, into three phases. Unfortunately, when they arrive they are a little disappointing. We call the stages early, middle and late. Perhaps Phillip Larkin's tripartite distinction of 'a beginning, a muddle and an end' might have been better.

Early adolescence

Early adolescence begins around the onset of puberty, which could be anywhere between nine and fourteen. It is usually described in language and imagery borrowed from the shipping forecast that interrupts urgently the radio programme you were listening to: storm clouds are gathering and tidal waves surging; there are tempests and floods. It is a liquid time of fluids and fluidity, of semen and blood. There is great turbulence of mood and emotion. The secure dams of the so-called 'latency years' have been burst open by the impact of puberty. There is tension and intensity, irritability and frenzy, and a driven quality as the inner turmoil seeks expression and discharge in its natural idiom of wild enactment and acting out. The secondary school youth is unrecognizable now, in radical discontinuity with the predictable child of primary school.

At the same time, however, according to Peter Blos (1962) and Harry Stack Sullivan (1973), early adolescence is a time when the special friend or 'chum' is of major significance. The friend may take on the previously idealized qualities of the parents, who are now – through the fear of incestuous breakthrough of Oedipal longings that may be realized in sexually maturing bodies – the object of disillusion and contempt. By the same token, these friendships may exhibit an intimacy of secrecy, and may be eroticized and sexualized. Displacement may take the form of crushes on older adolescents of the same or other sex, or adults outside the family. The peer group offers a sense of belonging and power that is no longer felt to be comfortably available within the family.

Middle adolescence

Middle adolescence is approximately the years between fourteen and seventeen. According to Blos, who first delineated these subphases, there is at this time a decline in the bisexuality, or 'transient homosexual practices', of early adolescence and the recognition of heterosexual tendencies that require a separation from the family and a final resolution of the positive Oedipus conflict (that is, the unconscious desire of the son for the mother, the daughter for her father), even though there will be fears of new dependencies at the point when dependence on the parents is beginning to decline.

Revolt against parental beliefs and values continues, and the peer group is largely the forum for the acquisition of standards and aspirations. It may be a time of idealism, experimentation and the challenging of moral and legal boundaries in anti-social behaviour. But the young person will also be more settled at times and easier to teach, and relative composure, with the capacity for compromise and empathy, return.

Late adolescence

The central psychological task for late adolescence is what Erik Erikson (1968) called 'identity formation'. This will involve a synthesis of sexual identity (which supposedly takes on a final form that is no longer easily reversible), social roles and personal identifications, with a decline in the experiences of inner crises, disorganizations and disunities.

The ego-deal, which is rooted in identification with the person and values of the same-sex parent, emerges as a new structure within the super-ego in late adolescence, and contains both individual and social components. It becomes the agency of aspiration and wish-fulfilment, and its function is to set personal challenges and punish by shame and loss of self-esteem.

Of course, even those of us who occasionally make use of these theories for ordering that which, fortunately, is unorderable, know that much of it is nonsense, especially the bits that imply a natural tendency towards monogamous heterosexuality. But this does not mean that it is not also in parts brilliant and inspirational. We need only to liberate it from its confinement to the years between short trousers and long skirts. Razumikhin, in Dostoyevsky's *Crime and Punishment*, makes sure our trainers stay firmly on the playground:

> Do you think I am blaming them for talking rot? Not a bit! I like people to talk rot. It's man's only privilege over the rest of creation. By talking rot, you eventually get to the truth. I'm a man because I talk rot. Not a single truth has ever been discovered without people first talking utter rot a hundred times or perhaps a hundred thousand times – and it's, in a way, a highly commendable thing even. But so far as we are concerned, you see, the trouble is that we can't even talk rot in our own way. Talk rot by all means, but do it in your own way, and I'll be ready to kiss you for it. For to talk nonsense in your own way is a damn sight better than talking sense in someone else's . . .

Identity vs normality

I am a child psychotherapist, and therefore I am often unclear and sometimes uncertain. But I draw an expert's salary, and occasionally catch myself using expressions like 'developmental timetables', committing myself to a view that there is an order in which people should do things. You know the sort of thing: 'Your child should be sleeping through the night by "x" months, ready to attend nursery by three years, school by five, and not leave home before eighteen (but be back by ten-thirty).' I am suspicious of this kind of talk. When I find myself compiling developmental sequences, it is usually in that mood of the good boy who has learned to sit still and not make too much noise.

I think we should approach these developmental timetables with that same sceptical air that we adopt when perusing those other timetables under the shattered glass at bus stops. They are not to be taken too seriously, but can serve to distract and occupy you while you wait to see what turns up. Often it is what you expect, but there can be some surprises.

The more serious and sinister side to any package of developmental stages is its authoritative imposition of a conformity. Holden Caulfield exclaims at one point in *Catcher in the Rye* (1958): 'I was probably the only normal bastard in the whole place – and that isn't saying much.'

It is, of course, never saying much to describe someone as 'normal', but sometimes we must admit when we are worried about ourselves or our children, it is the only word we are praying the doctor will pronounce.

The Latin word 'norma' meant 'square', an interesting anticipation of the slang used by the young in the second half of this century. The original square in question, however, was that of the carpenter, and until the early part of the nineteenth century the English word 'normal' referred to things that stood at a right angle to the ground. It was only in the 1840s that 'normal' acquired the meaning of conformity to a common type.

Today we make a different connection from that earlier one, but we still link normal and upright. We add value to geometry and come closer to 'upstanding' – always on the right lines. We use yardsticks to measure people so that those outside the lines can be labelled maladjusted, disabled, disordered or deviant and humiliated with their immaturity. It is not for nothing that we speak of 'arrests' in regard to developmental delay. Laws must be enforced and wrong-doers punished. The real criminal, however, we are relieved to hear, is not the poor child: somewhere in the background, orchestrating everything but submerged in alibi, are a Mr and Mrs Big, who over-indulged or neglected.

Prejudice can turn up in the most unexpected places. In work with sexually abused children, especially at the disclosure interview, some dolls are presented to which we refer as 'anatomically correct'. This expression supposedly draws attention to the extraordinary fact that most children's dolls are made without representation of the genitals, even though they always have at least two of everything else. But what do we want people with disabilities to make of this? Presumably, because this is what we actually believe, they have a body which is anatomically *incorrect* because the 'right body' has two legs, two arms, eight fingers, two thumbs, etc.

One version of Sigmund Freud believed that normal adult sexuality was a well-organized tyranny, no less so than any perversion. Norman O'Brown (1959) took up the idea and argued that all such organization, into, for example, heterosexuality, homosexuality and the rest of it, represented 'an exaggerated concentration on one of the many erotic possibilities present in the human body. In a non-repressive civilization', he argued, 'sexuality would be completely undifferentiated. Not only would all parts of the body share equally in the release of libidinal energy, but even the distinction between male and female would be insignificant.'

I will return to these ideas in a later chapter, but I want to stress here how this statement draws attention to an anxiety that is deeply pervasive in regard to identity. It is this anxiety, and the way we defend ourselves against it, that is the subject of this book on growing up. We can be greatly troubled by feelings of incoherence and internal contradiction, hating to be 'all over the place' and 'a mess'. This can lead us to over-value notions of consistency, and incline us powerfully to locate ourselves within fixed and predictable characters, relegating thereby our more fluid and flexibly various experiences of ourselves to developmental phases that are then outgrown and left behind.

We speak, for example, of early childhood as a time of temper tantrums, and assign perjoratively an infantile or regressive quality to this important experience of impatience and rage. Our implied and expressed contrast is with the reasonable composure of maturity. However, as the authors of *Gestalt Therapy* point out, it is not usually children who cannot wait: 'When temporarily frustrated of what he [sic] "knows" he will get, a small child screams and pounds. But then we see that when he gets the thing – or soon after – he is at once baffingly sunny' (Perls, Hefferline, Goodman, 1972). The scene created is a means of discharging tension, and this is exactly what 'waiting' is. Afterwards, therefore, the satisfaction is unspoiled, and the child can enjoy.

In general, it is the adult who cannot wait. We are frightened to make a scene and so our resentment and anger build up and we cannot then enjoy the thing when it comes. The experience is soured, as when the meeting in a restaurant we anticipated with excitement becomes the scene of a difficult tension or disagreement, and we discover we have eaten without noticing, without tasting. We are likely to be offended by the child's drama because we repress the similar tantrum in ourselves and are disturbed by this invitation to release it: 'What is here called maturity is likely neurosis. But if we think of the adults of Greek epic or tragedy or of biblical Genesis and Kings, we notice that they – not undistinguished for their intellect or sense of responsibility – did indeed carry on in a most "infantile manner".'

When I was eighteen and used to hitchhike, many drivers with expensive cars and suits used to tell me that when they were young they used to be Trotskyites. When I would ask them why they had changed, they would use expressions like 'real world', 'growing up' or 'commitments'. These were not patronizing or complacent people – they had after all taken a risk and taken me on trust from the side of a road. Perhaps they wanted to contact again something they had been separated from; to be in touch, to remember. But they did subscribe to the view that experimentation, idealism, rebellion and dissent were officially consigned to the adolescent years, as was a freer sexuality. I use the word 'officially' because perhaps they had personal and secret solutions to the restrictions we subject ourselves to in the name of maturity – private vices, drunken fighting, affairs.

I suppose I am more in the driving seat now, and try professionally to help other young people go where they want to go. Sometimes I give advice about what I think is the quickest or most interesting route; sometimes I may suggest another destination. This may not be everybody's idea about the best way to apply the insights of the psychoanalytic tradition, but I do hold to the view that psychotherapy with children and young people does not always have clearly defined goals such as the removal of symptoms. I agree 'that the most dismal science of all is the study of the "outcome" of psychotherapy', and that the work is 'a moral practice of a certain kind that people pursue because they value the life associated with it' (Kovel, 1981).

If psychotherapy is a moral enterprise, it will inevitably give content to good and evil, to right and wrong. The best aspect of this is an open declaration or manifesto of the sort of people we want to be and the sort of encounters with others we believe to be worthwhile. The less desirable temptation is, as we have seen, the assumption of expertise in the definition of what is normal or proper. Ivan Illich wrote that the profession of medicine, 'like all crusades . . . creates a new group of outsiders each time it makes a new diagnosis stick. Morality is as implicit in sickness as it is in crime and sin' (Illich, 1977). The same danger hovers in the wings of psychotherapy.

I prefer the alternative historical trend that regards the clients as active partners in the psychotherapeutic process. This replaces the arrogant assumption and attribution of sickness with notions of contribution and learning. What an individual learns may or may not be the same as that which is learned by someone else in an apparently similar situation. It may be different from what we want to teach.

Nevertheless, we have acquired a set of tools for living that we have found useful, and are looking to share them.

Somehow, these sorts of ideas seem at first sight to fit more comfortably with thoughts about psychotherapy and adults. After all, we grant adults the capacity to enter and leave contractual agreements, to acknowledge they have a problem and decide to do something about it. Furthermore, we have greater tolerance for the suffering of adults. Children have their whole lives ahead of them and we cannot bear them to be in pain. Parents may be cynical and resigned about their own compromises, levels of pain, distress, alienation or boredom, but will be by no means prepared to let their children suffer the same. With regard to the next generation, people seem always to have a higher standard than the one they are used to. This causes problems for everyone.

Torn up and in pieces

A fourteen-year-old girl was referred to me by a desperate father who could not stop talking about all the things his daughter had done wrong. He was at the end of his tether. The school was on the point of excluding her. He confessed, at my prompting, to a history of expulsions and failure in his own school career. He had as a teenager finally been sent away to a special boarding school, where the teachers had clung on with their fingernails to the skin of his teeth. He had survived, but at the price of regret and a pervading sense of missed opportunity. He was rich, being the owner of a successful building company he had established from nothing, but it meant very little to him. He felt uneducated and uncultured.

One of the things that exasperated this father most was his daughter's refusal to accept any of the charges levelled against her, by him or the school. He warned me she had refused to see me, but he was insisting, threatening withdrawal of something she really valued if she did not come. It was not hopeful as an individual psychotheraphy issue, and I tried to convey this but found myself talked out of my protests. I agreed to see her once on the understanding that further appointments would be her decision only. I hoped I might be in a better position to influence this man if he felt I had, in the first instance, taken on the problem in the way that he presented it.

She began by saying that she had not wanted to come to see me. There was no point. For the first few minutes I found it hard to free my thoughts from her father's words, 'She acknowledges nothing. She denies everything.'

I was angry with myself for allowing the sitution to arise. I had let myself be bullied and coerced out of a fear of the violence it had seemed I would have needed to unleash to get myself heard and have my opinion recognized. I had also felt sympathy for this worried but kind man who was clearly doing his best. These ruminations were enervating and distracting, tuning into familiar preoccupations and personal stories that exercise the most special fascination. It seemed a while before I remembered there was somebody else with me.

I began to realize that her expression was not, as I had first assumed, one of open defiance. It was more troubling, as though she were saying: 'This is my position, about which I am not certain. How could I be? But it just seems that way to me. And yes, my dad does worry. And yes, I am always in trouble.'

I tried a question: 'If you did not have to come here, if nobody was making you, what would you be coming for?' 'Nothing.' Her smile was hesitant, she did not want to give offence. I began to feel uneasy. It was not that I was the one who had to feel all the problems – there was no evacuation of that kind here, nor any clear way in which I could trace my rising discomfort to a simple wish of hers to rid herself of worry and pain. She looked as worried as I felt. My anxiety started to take shape.

Her father was bothered. The school was bothered. There did seem to be a big problem. What credibility would I have if I were to say that there was no problem! The source of the pressure was clear. How can you say what you think when the forces are lined up against you, shouting you down and drowning your protest? A similar conflict manifests itself frequently in the political arena. All people try to live their lives as best they can. If the authorities decide that the actions or way of life of a particular community should not continue and move in to confront, it will always be the community who gets the blame for the ensuing fight.

I noticed she was rustling a piece of paper in her pocket. She removed it, examined it for a moment, and then tore it in half. She tore it some more. She was persistent and determined, tearing this paper into smaller and smaller pieces with both hands, while trying to hold on to the bits. Some dropped on the floor. She tried to retrieve them.

I was hunting for metaphors by now, still mainly inside the problem, in search for something by way of a diagnosis that would keep the grown-ups at bay. But at the same time I was aware of a growing empathy and respect for this young woman as I saw her more closely. Perhaps she was after all tearing herself apart, or felt she was all torn up and in pieces. Perhaps there was a lot of sadness and these tears were tears.

There was something about gathering the bits of herself together, holding on to herself when everything seemed to be spilling out all over the place. Was this a statement about what she felt she had to do for herself in the absence of someone to share it all with? I was pleased she made no move to search for a bin to throw everything in, despite the amount. Or maybe this was indeed between the two of us, a displaced representation of an angry attack not apparent in her face or speech. She would like to tear me in shreds.

I asked her what the paper was. She said it was an advertisement someone had left under the windscreen wipers of the family car. She was clearly irate now: 'What a thing to do! If someone hands you something, you can say you don't want it, but if they just leave it on you or on something of yours, there is nothing you can do. You have to keep it.'

She was reminded of the day some catalogues were delivered through her door at home and the family threw them away. Some days later a lady called at the house to ask for them and was furious to find the family had disposed of them. 'But if someone forces you to have what you don't want, you don't have to keep it. You can do what you want with it. Can't you?'

1
Young People and Their Families

In the early 1980s we used to write that the central psychological subject in the study of adolescence was how young people and their families negotiated the process in which one of their number left home. This may need more than a little political revision in the mid-1990s, since we have managed to ensure in the external world that there are neither alternative homes nor meaningful employment opportunities for young people to move to. Psychologically, therefore, even though some questions are much the same, they are more difficult to ask. What does it mean to have your own home? Can you have a home without having a house to put it in?

Some of the most interesting advances of theory in psychiatry during the last thirty years have come from those who work with families on an out-patient basis. The word 'theory' comes from the Greek word 'theoria' and refers to the place from which a spectacle is viewed. In a similar vein, Freud thought that a common representation of a 'viewpoint' that often appears in dreams is the top of a tree, the high tree being a symbol of the desire to observe. In theory (or up a tree) a person can see everything that is going on below him but cannot himself be seen. Such protective distance may often feel necessary to students of the family, that scalding confine of proximity and overlap. Happily, for those of us who want to theorize but cannot bear to look, there is always philosophy to help cool us off when we are feeling hot and bothered about family life. In philosophy, said Karl Abraham, love is displaced from that which one *must* not see (the forbidden, incestuous aim is to be the participant–observer of one's parents' sexual intercourse) to that which one *cannot* see – one's own thoughts.

Certain philosophers have argued that people create prisons out of freedom. This cannot be right: prisons and freedom are created at the same time. We are frightened of being locked away, but frightened also of losing ourselves in the world of other people. And what we are frightened of has already happened. Prisons may seem a better option at times, where the walls and bars between us are clear. In any event, cells are familiar.

'Few would question that the innocent child was manufactured by Rousseau, with refinements by Wordsworth and a thousand lesser writers, interior decorators, and producers of greetings cards' (Kincaid, 1992). Before the eighteenth century, according to Philipe Aries (1962), there was no widespread belief in the state of childhood innocence, and no anxiety, therefore, about its possible corruption. Once invented, however, and linked to vulnerability, it evoked opposite notions of knowing power and defence. There was born the view which still persists, that 'the innocence needing protection is so feeble and is beset by foes so numerous and wily that any measures are justified, including putting innocence into protective custody or solitary confinement' (Kincaid, 1992).

Enter the nuclear family, or certain versions of it at least. If we grow up and live in secure units, parented and parenting in the style of warders, who, in the words of Leila Berg (1972), anxiously await a break-out, then adolescence is the time of Red Alert. However, it is of course not the family itself that is the problem, but rather the pressure that is exerted upon it. The abolition of society in the 1980s forced families into units of discreet and shivering isolation, anxiously suspicious of and jealously competitive with neighbouring specimens of the same type. Increasing responsibilities are piled on to parents at the same time that their support is eroded. Children and young people with no economic power of their own are bombarded by images on television about what sort of expensive consumer lifestyle they should feel entitled to assume. No wonder parenting feels sometimes, as the author Peter de Vries (1954) said, like feeding the mouth that bites you.

It should all be very different. George Bernard Shaw's thoughtful judgement that parenting ought to be watchful waiting – but mostly waiting, feels almost unattainable in the Age of Anxiety. We live in dread of a present future of increasing danger and diminishing opportunity that our vulnerable youngsters must be trained and disciplined to face down. This makes us submit more willingly to the imposition of standardized curriculi and comparative assessments of our school children.

Disability as exclusion

Parents and teachers have always been sensitive to the need to be aware of what children know, but the importance of understanding *how* individual children know what they know is implicitly discounted. We learn nothing about one child by testing another. And if it is still recognized that everybody learns in different ways and at different speeds, it is nevertheless more and more difficult to resist the idea that those who learn more slowly at school have something wrong with them and require 'remedial treatment'. It is a battle that people with disabilities and their families have been fighting for a long time, but in excluding them we have deprived ourselves of important knowledge.

'Disability', says Micheline Mason, from the Alliance for Inclusive

Education, 'was first thought of as a punishment and then, on the medical model, as an illness to be cured.' The aim always was 'normality', with the ready assumption that everybody knew what this was. A consequence was that the impairment became the focus of attention rather than the person who had it, as in the negative references to 'my Down's Syndrome son', etc.

The world that able-bodied people have created has speeded up the pace of life and values people only as producers who work outside their homes. It is a world of clocks and clocking-in. Disability to most of us means exclusion, and this is why we are frightened of it. As one representative of the excluded, it has become, in the way of other minorities, a container for the repudiated aspects of ourselves.

We project dependence onto people with disabilities as we do onto our children. We project our sweet nature and our fragility. In a continuing fantasy of damage, we are convinced that certain members of our community must be separated for their own good: they will be harmed by us; we are not trained; we are not what they need, as though, in a culture of experts, friendship counts for nothing. Worse, as compulsive caretakers, we imply that those we 'help' could never say what they want and need for themselves. They need us to define their needs for them.

Like little children, people with disabilities must be allowed no sexual feelings (although they are often exploited sexually) unless they are boys with learning difficulties, in which case they will be over-sexed and in need of segregation from 'vulnerable' girls. Unlike children, in our minds people with disabilities are never allowed to grow up. As Micheline Mason says:

> When I was eleven or twelve I realized that life was a competition in which I had very little chance, especially around boyfriends. In regard to pregnancy and sex education, there was massive ignorance about whether disabled people could have babies at all. Even if they could, it was felt that they should not because their children might then have a disability. It was impossible to believe that anybody could choose a disabled child.
>
> I did not go to school until I was fourteen. Until that time I had only seen able-bodied people. Nowhere did I see an image of myself grown up. There was an assumption that I would stay at home for ever. Books and television gave no access to disability. I saw no future and was blank about what kind of woman to be with no models around me.

In a leadership role, as mother and writer, Micheline Mason works within a self-advocacy movement which successfully challenges concepts towards people with disabilities, physical and learning, which has profound implications for the lives of all families and our need for community:

> I always wanted my daughter to feel that the world is as much hers as anyone else's. She must be given opportunities to develop as far as she can, aware of the oppression that works to restrict her. She needs relationships with other people who are different from her and from whom she can expect co-operation. She must be allowed to be powerful, to direct herself. She needs to see disabled people having a good life and achieving what they want. There is nothing wrong with her. There is nothing wrong with the way she looks. She needs to stay part of the ordinary community.

Family therapy

We need her to stay with us as well. Our fragmented community stays fragile because it excludes the parts of itself it fears. Children vanish from our midst into special and boarding schools, irrespective of the impact on siblings, friends and everyone else. Old people disappear into homes for the elderly. Maybe we are frightened it will be our turn next, but in any event we begin and continue the process of exclusion, when, as internal exile, we send our 'naughty' children to their rooms.

Family therapy, with its links to organizational, group and systems theories, and its insistence on the important coherence of parts to the whole, has contributed greatly to the understanding of processes such as scapegoating. Equally valuable is its disinclination to view the person expressing the symptom as the one with the problem.

Christopher

> Many years ago a colleague asked me to join him in working with a family he had been seeing for a while and about whom he felt very stuck. We agreed he would say nothing beforehand about their presenting problem, as he was interested to see what a newcomer would make of it.
>
> Half an hour into the session, I was thinking that this family therapy stuff certainly beat working. It was a grey winter's day, but it felt like the sun was shining right into the room. Two parents were speaking eloquently about themselves and their family, while their sixteen-year-old son, Christopher, sat between them, looking admittedly rather sad, but politely agreeing whenever he was brought into the conversation, and attracting no special attention. A younger sibling drew pictures on the low table.
>
> Suddenly, or so it seemed to me, my colleague pointed out that

nobody was talking about Christopher's serious suicide attempt some weeks previously, which had been the presenting problem at the time of the original referral. The parents smiled benignly and said something to the effect that it was all forgotten now – Christopher had just been a bit upset at the time. I felt almost sick with anxiety, the more so because of the non-caring air of ease I had been enjoying moments previously. It was clear that something was very wrong with this family's alarm system. I had experienced first hand how powerfully insensitive it was to signals of distress and the brutally numbing and paralyzing consequences of its system of denial. It was little wonder that a family member had felt he needed to do something drastic to draw concerned attention to himself.

Thinking about young people in their families moves the so-called adolescent transition away from purely intrapsychic approaches. Typically, these latter perspectives tend to focus on identity formation, the conflict between dependence and autonomy, gender identity and intimacy with peers. Yet it is always as if the young people are emerging from a static family context, whose impact is largely felt within the young people themselves. It is of course true that throughout life many people are constantly trying to examine and modify their relationships to the values and prohibitions of their parents that have become second nature to them, seeking to revise and recast them from within. For some this may be a task especially undertaken at the point of application to become a member of adult society – the best club in town.

But adolescents are not isolates who react solely to the demands of their inner impulses. They are members of ongoing family systems which continue to exert open and hidden influences on them, and which they in turn continue to influence. Whatever physiological and psychological changes are happening for young people will be in continuing interaction with the behaviour and attitudes of those around them. Parents who have discouraged difference and individuation in their children and each other may struggle immensely when their teenagers turn away from the family for their excitement and support. It is possible that such parents may not have had good experiences in their own families when young:

Mrs White

Mrs White had witnessed many rows between her parents when she was a girl, and had often seen her father beating her mother. She had always thought herself to be the rejected child in her family of origin because she felt her parents preferred her brother. As a child she had longed always for a closer relationship with her father, who she felt to be distant and cold.

When Mrs White had her second child, Timothy, his name was put on the at-risk register at birth because of several incidents of physical abuse inflicted by Mr White on Timothy's three-year-old brother. Perhaps because of this Mr White rejected Timothy from the very beginning, and would have nothing to do with him. Both boys were taken into voluntary care when Timothy was six, at the time when Mr and Mrs White separated. Mrs White married another man shortly afterwards, but this relationship proved also to be stormy and violent. There were frequent fights between the couple, and on two occasions Timothy called the police to stop a raging battle. The second marriage was also unstable in that both partners were always talking about separating, establishing a pattern of leaving and reuniting.

Timothy came to the attention of the child psychiatry services because of his worrying combination of a rather perverse sexualization of his contact with female teachers at his school, and his threats of violence towards them. What began as ordinary requests from Timothy for help or attention from the female staff at his school would culminate in the women feeling they had been drawn into a masturbation fantasy that left them feeling disgusted and abused. Their understandable reluctance to approach Timothy would then lead to his furious protests at their distance, and these outbursts had a quality of real menace. With male teachers Timothy would politely convey that he required no assistance.

Mrs White knew she had always been very attached to Timothy, and thought she probably identified heavily with him as the child who was both rejected and witnessed violence between parents. She probably also involved him unconsciously in her search to produce an intensely close relationship between a parent and a child, in the attempt to satisfy the unmet need from her own past. To this extent it was difficult for her to allow Timothy any kind of separate life, regarding him as a part of herself. She admitted to being possessive and controlling, and dreaded the possibility that he might one day find a girlfriend. It was also likely that in the periodic absences of Mrs White's partners Timothy would be drawn seductively into a compensating comfort role for his mother, only to be dropped at their return.

It was as though Mrs White believed that if she could prevent Timothy from leaving home, she could somehow alleviate the historic pains and neglect of her own childhood. Timothy's feared separation from her threatened to reawaken the despairing loneliness and sense of abandon she had felt as a little girl.

Timothy was playing his part loyally. His relationships with his female teachers was an exact recreation of that between himself and his mother. In this way he defended himself against any possible rising anxiety that he was ever separate from her. He needed always to involve the women in his sexual fantasies because then his mother, as represented by these teachers, would always know what he was up to, even what he was thinking. He must have no secrets, because this would be to concede an apparently impermeable barrier between them. It was as if he was saying, 'My mother is always checking up on me, therefore she must always know what I am doing. She muddles the relationships of care and sex, and therefore I sexualize those between myself and my carers. I am tantalized and then dropped, and thus act out my rage when my teachers withdraw. My mother is loved by violent men. My attacks will confirm my love and win her (them) back.'

Timothy's stepfather, Mr Davenport, had never known his own parents and had grown up in children's homes. He was trying his best to assemble a composite notion of a caring relationship from those pieces of reliable concern he had received from the best of the staff who had looked after him in the past. He alternated between a bewildered incomprehension about the needs of his wife and stepson, and an extremely idealized view of a family in a state of siege that would stay together for ever and take on the whole world.

The combination of this latter mood of Mr Davenport, and Mrs White's usual attitudes that she struggled to keep in check, was devastating. For Timothy both parents would paint a terrifying picture of life outside the front door with its dangers of crime, drugs and sexually promiscuous women who carried diseases, accused young men of rape, or became pregnant to force marriage on unwilling partners. If Timothy were to appear interested in befriending somebody of either sex, that unfortunate person would be mercilessly attacked or ridiculed. In the same way, neither Mr Davenport nor Mrs White had any friends of their own. Mr Davenport had a job in which he felt undervalued and badly treated. Mrs White rarely went out.

Clearly the odds were stacked heavily against these parents managing alone to help their young son make a life of his own without cutting him off completely in an act of retaliation for what would be felt as his betrayal and abandonment.

But which of us can hear the personal decision of a loved one and not experience true loneliness? To stand out of the way in another's life, when that person makes a choice that excludes us, and to remain without resentment emotionally available and within communicable distance, is very difficult to manage in close relationships. When unresolved grief over chronic or cumulative losses in the past meets with a meaningless adult life of isolation and alienation in the present, it may feel next to impossible:

> They fuck you up, your mum and dad.
> They may not mean to, but they do.
> They fill you with the faults they had
> And add some extras, just for you. (Larkin, 1974)

Linda

Linda is seventeen. She likes to talk to people – or, more accurately, she likes herself to talk – and be where others are talking. She does not like to listen. When I say something, her eyes glaze over. Unusually for me, I am unable to feel hurt by this apparent disregard, because I am so charmed by the look of complete contentment that is on her face. When I draw her attention to the situation, she is embarrassed, but concedes at once. 'When you speak,' she says, 'it is like a fan heater blowing warm air towards me.'

That is one way of putting it. I suppose I should be pleased the air I talk is not hot, although at best the comment damns me with faint praise. It looks to me, however, as though Linda seeks repeatedly the reassurance of establishing that she can have her own thoughts in private without the anxiety of being alone. Each time I speak, she enjoys further confirmation of the fact that I do not know what she is thinking. I am the parent who reads the riot act, or the bedtime story, while Linda remembers what she did with her friends and plans for repetition or change.

And there is another thing. Linda's friends, by her own account, are not quite what one would have expected. They are always people she does not like very much. My explanation of this, which takes into account the way she ensures that nothing much can come from her relationship with me, is that in this way she magically realizes the wish, by living it out, that all connection between people will lack excitement and passion and lead to no productive outcome. It is an envious attack on her parents' sexual relationship. When she shuts up shop as I approach, she becomes the woman she would like her mother to be – closed, impenetrable and contentedly self-contained. Furthermore, in keeping her dull friends close to her, she prevents them from doing anything exciting with anyone else. Conversely, as she confessed, she imagines others view her in the same way, and she feels claustrophobic anxieties when others seek to make relationships with her.

It is this last admission from Linda that moves us on. After one session of extreme tedium for me, in which she is talking more and listening less than usual, I ask her why she pretends to be boring. She looks stunned. Encouraged by a different reaction from her usual one, I follow up with two right jabs: 'Who would be most affected if you allowed yourself to be more exciting? What would be the catastrophe?' In ducking under her defences, I manage to provoke a retaliative outburst that surprises her as much as it does me. 'My mother, my father, my brother.' She becomes visibly different, suppressing an impulse to cry or shout by tensing the muscles in her neck. But whatever she is trying to choke off is sticking in her throat. She is clearly tasting what she can not swallow. The emotion will not be suppressed.

Linda had been a high-flyer at school until six months previously. Since that time she had done little work, and had failed important exams that she had been expected to pass with distinction, along the path mapped out to university and a professional career. A series of family interviews made clear what had been going on for a long time.

Linda's mother had looked to her daughter to be her champion, her conquering heroine, who would bring credit on her and outstrip the accomplishments of her competitively successful husband. The only area of achievement for Linda's mother that the marriage partners collaborated to permit, was in bringing up the children and running the home. She needed to be the perfect mother, but in order for this to be the case, she needed to have perfect children.

It was a trap. To keep her mother's love, Linda felt she had to be an exemplar, an ideal. To fail was to court the risk of losing her mother's love. To succeed was to risk losing, by overtaking and leaving behind her father and her under-achieving younger brother. But to succeed was also to lose herself to her mother.

Linda's parents bound her inextricably to them by driving her to live out their aspirations. She was to be the triumphant woman through whom her mother could vicariously flourish, or for her father the selfless and adoring female, happily settled in second place.

Probably Linda had always felt like some kind of mannequin or doll. Perhaps her brother, under similar pressures, was rebelling earlier. But it was clear that the imminent separation that the family was facing as Linda became a young woman had provoked a more urgent crisis. At such times older adolescents can often feel tremendous guilt at thinking of themselves as centres of their own initiative, and unexpected failure may well be the expression of such guilt, taking the form of self-defeating attempts at detachment.

For Linda, none of the options that it was assumed she would want to pursue felt like choices of her own; they seemed more like capitulation to the desires and needs of her parents. Her negative attempt to resolve the conflict by failure and boredom was nevertheless a creative family compromise. She made some distance for herself by refusing to succeed for her mother and declining to be contentedly ordinary for her father, but kept the family together by remaining a source of concern to them both. This allowed her mother and father to stay in their role as parents, providing and caring for their daughter, who had made it impossible for herself to leave.

Adoption

All parents are foster parents, wrote Kahlil Gibran. All children are fostered. We, however, live within another network of meaning, and theorize a difference between those families who think of themselves as fostering or adoptive, and those who do not.

Andrew and Mary

Mr and Mrs Bowen know what I mean. Mr Bowen hurled us all, unself-consciously, into the very heart of the matter with his opening complaint. 'We feel that Andrew does not belong to us any more.'

Andrew was adopted at the age of two along with his sister Mary, who was two years older. Mr and Mrs Bowen said they had tried to have 'our own children' for many years but without success. From the outset, Mary had been a challenging and headstrong girl who had repeatedly been in trouble at school. Now, aged eighteen, the parents were worried her behaviour had taken a more delinquent turn. She was involved with a group of young people who were taking drugs; she seemed always to have different boyfriends, and she had recently been arrested for shoplifting.

The parents were astonishingly open. It was as though the obvious pain of their present lives had taken them beyond any ability or desire to dissemble. 'We never really thought of Mary as *ours*. She was already so much herself when we adopted her, so set and determined in her ways and demands. She never really seemed to accept us, never allowed us to feel good about ourselves or what we were giving her.'

In all the years of their urgently summoned attendance, at the inevitable meetings of crisis and warning in the offices of a succession of head teachers, Mary would sometimes look from one to the other of her adoptive parents in bewilderment, as if genuinely unsure what they were doing there. It was clear Mr and Mrs Bowen cared deeply for Mary – she made it impossible not to be thinking and worrying about her all the time – but she was like a stranger to them. 'If the truth be told, we have always been a little frightened of her.'

Andrew by contrast had been loving and affectionate from the beginning. In nursery and primary school he would run excitedly towards whichever of his parents had come to collect him and leap into their arms. He preferred laps to chairs, and enjoyed games and stories. He loved to go on family outings and holidays, and Mr and Mrs Bowen felt always greatly moved by the trust and appreciation he managed to squeeze into the simple names he gave them – 'Mummy' and 'Daddy'.

Recently, however, Andrew had changed. He had become foul-mouthed and abusive at school, and ungrateful and defiant at home. He was seeking out the company of friends of whom his parents did not approve, and who they felt were a bad influence. He would disappear for long periods of time with these friends, returning home late, and with the smell of cigarettes and alcohol on his breath. He was increasingly sullen and surly, barely acknowledged his parents' presence except to disparage contemptuously whatever moves they made towards him, and shared nothing of his own life.

Moreover, Mr and Mrs Bowen were very worried about the effect that Mary was having on Andrew. Their relationship had changed on Andrew's part from a polite indifference to a devoted and admiring adherence, and the parents thought Mary exercised considerable power over Andrew that was pulling him away from them.

I picked up the theme of influence – malign, powerful and unseen – of Mary and the unsuitable friends, and asked them if they could say something more. Mrs Bowen knew what I was looking for. 'I always worried about the quality of parenting the two children had received before they came to us. We were told by the social workers that the mother was very young and rather wild, and that the children's father was a drifter who disappeared for long periods of time, and was seemingly on the fringes of criminal activity. I don't think there was ever any violence in the home, just deprivation and chaos. I have the impression there was constant partying, and that the children had little protection from the noisy comings and goings of lots of different young people.'

She is troubled by the possibility that heredity, or the early environment, may be superior in strength, in terms of the determination of developmental outcome, to the many years of consistent care that she and her husband have given. She knows I could not possibly have the answer to her question, but she asks it all the same. 'Which will exert the greater influence in the end?' But there are other questions to ask. What does it mean to influence another person, and why is this something that we want? 'There is no such thing as a good influence, Mr Gray,' says Lord Henry in Oscar Wilde's novel, *The Picture of Dorian Gray.* 'Why?' 'Because to influence a person is to give him one's own soul. He does not think his natural thoughts, or burn with his natural passions. His virtues are not real to him. His sins, if there are such things as sins, are borrowed. He becomes an echo of someone else's music, an actor of a part that has not been written for him.'

It is, of course, a central theme of Winnicott's work: 'the intricate dialectic between contact and differentiation' (Greenberg and Mitchell, 1983), 'the separation that is not a separation but a form of union', (Winnicott, 1974).

From the point of view of parents, it is rare that situations regarding children present themselves in the form of clear and present dangers, like running into the road or swallowing bleach. A protective parental attitude communicates the anxieties of the parents. The best structures inside which our young can grow are permissive, in order that they can act without fear, shame or resentment, and learn by their mistakes. For ourselves, our best opportunity is a culture of firm parental morals and continuing personal interests and aspirations. The point for everybody is surely how we ourselves behave, not how our young should or must conduct themselves. This has the advantage of offering young people in times of confusion and anxiety something with which they can play or experiment for themselves. It protects them from the pressure of being compelled to dance in somebody else's place, to somebody else's tune.

'Children cannot be taught to grow,' wrote Susan Isaacs (1930, 1933), '. . . all one can do is provide a rich soil for exploration and development.' This is true. The problem is, that when you say things like this you tend to attract a certain level of alarm around you (somebody once described Malting House, the school in Cambridge for children aged two to ten that Isaacs founded, as a 'pre-genital brothel').

Adoption throws many of these questions and issues into sharp relief. In growing up, all children have to contend with the disillusionment they feel with their parents, and the disappointments they see or imagine that their parents feel in them. It is such concerns as these that can generate fantasies like the 'family romance', in which a child may believe herself to be the real child of other parents than the ones she has – royalty, perhaps, or other celebrities of her culture.

A child's self-image will be constructed from her experiences in relationship to the parents who care for her. When her parents seem dissatisfied with her, she *may* be able to distinguish the times of their understandable exasperation with her from what is clear failure or weakness in them. She may also conclude, however, that she herself is a person who does not deserve good care; that if her parents are dissatisfied with her, she must be in important ways unsatisfactory. The internal representation of herself will be further complicated by her own feelings of hatred and envy, which may give rise to unconscious fantasies of essential qualities of badness within her.

Such universal experiences as these emphasize the continuum between the concerns of those children who grow up in their families of origin and those who are fostered or adopted. Within a family that stays together, however, unless there is sustained abuse, cruelty or neglect, the child will have the opportunity to modify the way she thinks about herself. She can balance and offset the moment-to-moment feelings of rejection with the experiences of feeling loved, of forgiving and being forgiven.

It may be very different for children who are adopted. The existence of their 'other parents' is no fantasy of family romance, but has the status of a fact, communicated to them by powerful adult figures from whom they construct their view of themselves and the world. Inevitably, adopted children will generate some ideas about what their birth parents were like, building this picture from the amalgamation of the information they are given and their current feelings about their adoptive parents. They will also try to tackle the disturbing question as to why these first parents 'gave them up', and it is in this area that the fusion of the child's unconscious fantasies with those of her carers can combine to make adoption a convenient organizer for other conflicts.

The important question to address when children are moved from their birth parents is, what is the affective meaning of the adoption story, in the minds of the children, adoptive parents and wider society? In other words, it is not the fact of adoption itself that is significant, but what the parties involved think it means, presently and retrospectively.

> Mr and Mrs Bowen admitted that they had never really grieved the lost ideal of themselves as what they used to call 'real parents'. Mr Bowen felt that the discovery of his infertility some years previously had been a devastating blow to his masculinity: 'I thought of myself as not a proper man – just a kid.' He also struggled to believe that his wife could ever really respect him, and feared she must secretly regret having married him. He thought that any row or tension between them on any subject at all was in fact the displaced expression of this larger resentment.
>
> Both parents felt a mixture of envy and furious despair at the casual and irresponsible ease with which they imagined the birth parents of their adopted children had conceived. This was a clear fantasy of their own as they admitted they had no way of knowing

the true picture. Another idea that troubled Mr Bowen was that the children were the product of a wild and promiscuous sexuality, a projection of his own dreams, viciously repressed by the narcissistic blow of his sterility. This caused particular problems in his relationship with Mary, whom he always invested with the same kind of sexuality, and against which he felt unprotected in the absence of the incest barrier.

Mr Bowen felt he had always failed his adopted daughter Mary because of his inability to be relaxed with her, or to challenge or confront her. In all of these situations of intimate contact he could not remove the thought of the sexual possibilities from his mind. He therefore withdrew and left her care and discipline to his wife.

Probably both parents were unable to affirm and celebrate Mary's sexual experimentation because it was a painful contrast with what they felt to be the unproductive nature of their own, and this may have left them feeling angry with her. In this respect they may have been close to the commonly observed difficulty of parents in all families, who feel forced to suffer what they perceive as the fresh and unrestrained excitement of their teenagers' burgeoning sexuality, at a time when their own sexuality may be diminishing in terms of interest and intensity. Where this is the case, there are better solutions for all concerned than enviously attacking the young, in whatever subtle guise this may be done.

Mr and Mrs Bowen worked hard to counter a strong pull in themselves to split the children in their care into the 'good child Andrew' and 'the bad child Mary'; or 'our two good children' and 'the two bad children of the bad birth parents'. Sometimes, even though it was a false solution, the splitting enabled them to cope better with the anxiety the children brought upon them as a consequence of the difficult behaviour outside the home. 'We were able to say to ourselves that nobody could really blame us because they are not our own children.' On good days, this perspective allowed a certain distance from the children's problems which lead to speedier resolution. On bad days it was used in the service of self-attack, as a painful reminder that these were not their children because they could not have their own childen.

Work with Mr and Mrs Bowen was directed to supporting them in their resolve to hold on to their understanding of what was happening for all members of the family. Mary and Andrew were experimenting with behaviour that was based on ideas about what they and their adoptive parents thought their birth parents were like. They were trying to get to know the people who brought them into the world by doing what they thought those people would do. But these ideas about their birth parents would in addition be derived

> from the dominant cultural views that are held about unmarried mothers and irresponsible fathers; about young people in general and the dangers for all of us of sexuality. The current intolerance of single parents, as if they were doing something wrong, is a certain indication of uneasy conscience, of the effort it costs to suppress forbidden temptations and tendencies. Condemnation of those who 'give up' their children for adoption is the same.
>
> The self-doubt and contempt felt by Mary and Andrew had coalesced around the definition of themselves as 'adopted children', which reduced their lives to the single act of their 'relinquishment' by their first parents. This gave apparent substance or reality to vague but probably universal feelings of being unworthy or unlovable. To that extent, Mary's whole life with Mr and Mrs Bowen, and Andrew's recent delinquent rebellion, could be understood as a dramatization of the whole adoptive process. They sought urgent answers to questions that troubled them at the very centre of their lives: 'Are we so bad that everyone gives up on us, as you tell us and we believe our birth parents did? Or is there a love that is stronger, and that can prove itself by not rejecting us, whatever we do?'

I add this. We parents, foster and adoptive included, are close to children because we love them. The language of loving affinity, however, is shot through with the values and concepts that derive from the prevailing arrangements of property. To prove and satisfy our love we believe it is necessary to own its object, to have and to hold. There is created as a consequence a category of the disowned or discarded, which is the final carrier of negative valence. Into this abyss fall the divorced and jilted, the unemployed and redundant, the fostered and adopted; objects, these, of fearful pity. But at this depth of experience there is another expression of love to remember that helps to reframe the adoption story. Other people are not ours to give. In any event, giving to is not the same as giving up.

2
Adolescents in Their Own Minds

> 'It's ridiculous the way people are appointed to jobs,' Charlie was saying. 'Surely it should happen at random? People in the street must be approached and told that they are now editor of *The Times* for a month. Or they are to be judges, or police commissioners, or toilet attendants. It has to be arbitrary. There can be no connection between the appointment and the person unless it is their utter unsuitability for the position. Don't you agree?'
>
> 'Without exception?' enquired the Fish, languidly.
>
> 'No. There are people who should be excluded from high position. These are people who run for buses and put their hands in their pockets to ensure their change dosn't jump out. There are other people who have suntans that leave white patches on their arms. These people should be excluded, because they'll be punished in special camps' (Kureishi, 1990).

When Sally wishes to indicate 'herself', she points usually to the centre of her chest. Sometimes she makes an outward curving gesture with her arms, palms upraised, which is accompanied by a slight inclination of her body. I notice that she never points to her head, stomach or genitals, nor to her open mouth, the place from where her speech is coming.

William James believed that a person's innermost self resided chiefly in a series of movements in her head and neck. But orbiting this central self, this self of selves, like the sun and its planets in the solar system, there is a medley of subsidiary selves. Each of these is, in turn, complex.

That certainly is how it feels. Furthermore, we know there is often conflict between and among our actual and potential selves. William James himself (-selves) apparently wanted to be a priest and a pirate, a dandy and a professor, a philosopher and a ladies' man, but thought these to be incompatible: 'The philosopher and the lady-killer [sic] could not dwell together in the same tenement of clay.' Karl Abraham (1913) could have told him why that was as we've seen. Actually, the life of James shows that he did try out a number of possible selves and did not until relatively late in his life construct the apartment building by which he is most widely renowned. Some clay, that!

These ideas resonate in the political field with the vision of Karl Marx. In a socialist future a person may be a hunter, a writer or farmer in the morning, without needing to be any of these things in the afternoon. But is this all, socialism included, just the stuff of which Charlie's adolescent dreams are made? Something to be grown out of, as we leave behind our Lego-youth, and close on completion the front door of our brick house, overlooked for the rest of our lives by the bank or building society?

Sally says an interesting thing one day, which gets me jumping. 'I don't think I'm having an adolescence.' Now, hold on a minute, I want to say, but keep instead a hold on myself. I resist the urge to put my hand over my identity badge, 'Child and Adolescent Psychotherapist', the third word of which feels like it is in flashing lights. Is she making fun of me? Is she here under false pretences? I am sure I read somewhere that adolescence is the social and psychological adjustment to puberty. In fact I have said that exact same thing myself at many lectures and seminars. It is obvious to me that Sally's body is changing – she is no longer in short trousers. So what is she talking about?

Fortunately, the discipline of many years of professional training ensures that these panic stations remain unknown to my interlocutor. I am on the outside, as always, impassive and inscrutable. A man without training would have fainted, or blurted the whole lot out. Instead, from somewhere within me, a polite request is heard: 'Would you like to say something more about that?' Before she can answer, at least as far as this book is concerned, I am hearing a similar story from Gary, although his, at the age of twenty-five, is cast in retrospective regret. Adolescence was something he never had.

Sally alternates between moods of worry and anger. She either feels there is something terribly wrong with her because she is not feeling and living in the way that she is supposed to at the age of sixteen, or she is enraged at being pressured by typecast, excluded by both peers and elders, who think she should be behaving like all her friends do; except, as she thinks about it, she is not sure her friends are behaving like adolescents either.

Defining adolescence

For many years commentators have rightly challenged the view that adolescence is inevitably a troubled and stressful time. Psychoanalysts had told tales of deep distress and insecurity; of moody egotism and morbid melancholy; of imagined ill-health, or denial of the body, with flights into the lofty spaces of intellectual abstraction. Adolescence was a frantic rave-scene of drugs and alcohol that only the middle-aged analysts could see. All around them young lithe bodies writhed in sexual excess, pausing briefly to hurl bricks at authority, or perpetrate further acts of danger and personal risk, before going back to the sex.

Anthony Clare (1974) had an amusing caricature of this kind of approach:

> When he's not anxiously examining his well-used penis in front of the mirror for worrying signs of wear and tear, the adolescent male is driving its flamboyant substitute, Dad's shiny car, at 'penetrating' speeds, to the shock and consternation of his adapted and adjusted parents. When not provocatively displaying her undies to her troubled Dad in the bathroom (adolescence is a bad time for Dads), the adolescent female is yielding in a drunken stupor to an acne-spotted loafer, whose name and face, if not the rest of him, is forgotten by the following melancholic morning.

Researchers may have written of a much smoother transition between adolescence and adulthood, but the psychoanalysts have had more fun. The problem is, this 'stormy adolescence' has quite an appeal, and is the theory that underpins the commercial exploitation of young people. It sells newspapers and magazines to fascinated and horrified adults, and boosts attendances before television and cinema screens.

Two surveys, for example, of the way newspapers report adolescence found that the typical young person to appear in the press is 'criminally inclined (though a sport lover) and likely to be murdered or injured in an accident' (Falchikov, 1989). What will be the effect on young people, to see these images of themselves 'reflected' back with such pervasive persistence? What subtle or gross distortion does the daily trickle or torrent of such portrayals implant in the minds of the newspaper-reading, television-watching adult, to influence the perception and treatment of the young? Who can see groups of young men and not tense up in anticipation of attack? Or any gathering of young people in the street, without thoughts of vandalism, solvent abuse or delinquency?

> Alas, in our present Western culture . . . puberty and adolescence is a period which brings much suffering into the lives of young people and their parents, a period of turbulence instead of sparkle. Partly this is due to the persistence in some quarters of an idiotic guilt about matters biological. . . . Partly also – *and the part is a great one* – to the vicious manipulation of adolescents by media and market forces anxious only to obtain as much money as possible, at whatever cost in physical and mental health (James Tanner in Buckler, 1987).

Puberty is a fact of the body and our bodies are the closest we get to nature. But we humans are born with drives or instincts that are weak because, unlike our animal cousins, we have no rigid pre-adaptation to reality. For us, socialization replaces instinct. Paradoxically, the consequences turn out to be the same. We find ourselves as rigidly bound in our behaviour by the symbolic 'instinctivization' of our cultures as are animals by their biological instincts. We are trained, as children, to *want* to do what our society says we *must*. We earn our esteem, as boys or girls, by trudging along the fixed and determined channels that are dug out for us. Later, as men and women, we willingly continue to propagate a whole cultural system that keeps us enslaved.

Adolescence, the social and psychological adjustment to puberty, occupies a central and unique position in all of this. As prescribed excess, it is the carnival of the catholic calendar, the time to let your hair down ('puberty', incidentally, derives from the Latin word meaning 'hairy'). Children have to go to school; grown-ups have to go to work. These are the extended Lenten episodes of personal hardship, sacrifice and restraint. In between is party-time, the safety valve, and anything goes. 'It is the best time of their lives and they had better enjoy it', is the way we think about it, in order that they remind us that there *is* another life, and show their gratitude for our bounteous generosity, albeit ambivalently bestowed. As Joe Orton's 'parent' says: 'Every luxury was lavished on you – atheism, breast feeding, circumcision. I had to make my own way' (Orton, 1967).

The pressure-release called adolescence brings other pressures in its wake. It may be a matter of irresistible biology that every individual succumbs, eventually, to breast areolar growth or jumping-jack flash, but there is no instinctual idea that informs us of what to expect. For that we look to the predominant images of the society in which we live. Furthermore, as we shackle our young into their age-bands of chronology, and decide what every seven, ten or thirteen year old should be like, 'nature' is in the changing rooms, laughing at the tricks it plays on us.

> Growth changes have much more in common from one child to another when related to the phase of puberty (what might be called their 'physical' age) rather than to their actual age. Some normal [sic] girls will show their first features of puberty as early as nine, others not until fourteen; some will menstruate before eleven, others not until sixteen. Some normal boys begin to develop as early as ten, others as late as sixteen . . . In many respects children who are of the same stage of pubertal development . . . have more in common than those of the same 'chronological' age.

This being the case, we can understand why young people worry so much about themselves and their development, taught as they are to assess their own situation by comparing it with the person next to them.

There is no constant feature of 'normal' puberty. There is no right order of the events of puberty and variation is great. There is no standard duration in the progress of specific features or the overall complete course from start to finish. In some children the whole process may be completed in . . . two years, in others it may take over five, but it depends also on how completion of puberty is defined. Maturity, in terms of the capacity of the individual to have a child of his own, need not relate directly to the extent of physical maturity that might be implied by certain of the pubertal changes. Body hair, for example, can continue to develop for many years into adult life, long after reproduction is possible; conversely, the onset of menstruation in girls, is an event which usually precedes actual fertility by several months (Buckler, 1987).

Communicating selves

Sally keeps a diary. This is something young people sometimes take up around her age. Her diary is her secret confidant, the one to whom anything can be told without fear of reproach, without shame. It is an aspect of her mother and father, one of their moods. Perhaps it recalls for Sally experiences of unconditional love, and is the persistence of the wish for that response in present daily search. But this diary is no mother of early infancy, no father who knows how his daughter feels, without her having to speak. It holds her memories, but knows nothing until it is told. And it does not presume. Nor does it intrude.

Sally's diary serves as an important outlet for her emotional life. We could say that it indicates a capacity within her for communication between and among her various selves. She can listen to, learn from and be surprised by the things she finds herself feeling or saying. But these thoughts and emotions need to take external shape. They have to be located outside of her, in another form and place. They must furthermore be locked up and hidden, to keep them safe. From what? 'I am terrified that someone will find my diary and read what I have written. It is not only that I would be embarrassed. It is more than that. I would feel that what was in my diary would no longer be mine if anyone else were to see it.'

She is talking about ownership and loss, about the wishes and fears around separation and differentiation. In point of fact, Sally is certain that her parents would in no circumstances open and read anything of hers that is private. She must, then, be frightened of her own wish to be known, which she fears would spell the loss of her individuality, her very identity. The ceremonies of her diary express her ambivalence. She continues to demonstrate the existence of her secret self while flirting with the possibility of its seizure, its (stolen) access to others. It is the best she can do.

The work of Margaret Mahler (1975) and Donald Winnicott (1958, 1965) emphasized the continuities between notions of intra- and extrauterine life, and postulated for the baby in the period immediately after birth a stage of undifferentiation and merger, out of which the ego and the self emerged through processes of gradual differentiation and separation. Today, with the developments in the Kleinian tradition, which has always maintained that the ego is present from the beginning, and the researches of Daniel Stern (1985) and others, the consensus is probably that the infant is prestructured from birth to differentiate and separate, and that there are no clear-cut phases of development. The linear model is replaced by a helix, and it is acknowledged that several progressions or advances can happen at the same time.

Despite this, it must still be the case that at the beginning there is no first person singular to evoke and express the infant's subjectivity. There are clearly moments of burgeoning self-experience, the dawning recognition of a world of other people, but on the whole the assumption is that the infant has yet to establish relatively stable self and other attributes.

At no time in our lives, of course, are we completely separate from our families, friends and enemies. It is rather the case that we always situate in other people or entrust to them any number of our psychological or emotional selves. Other people treat us in the same way. Nevertheless, we assume there to be a notional stage in early life when a border or boundary fence is erected, a time when the subject takes on the identity that has been allocated to him.

'The "I" sets in as an identifying inner agent: "This is me." ', writes Joel Kovel (1981), of those early moments of the first individuation. The process is not defined in any clearcut way but will comprise, broadly speaking, the internalization of many of the beliefs, habits, values, preferences and opinions of the carers.

For young children, this may not seem or feel conflictual. Ideas or attitudes may be happily taken over from the parents and their representatives, or happily contradicted. There will not be much of a doubt about the young child's gender identity, in her own mind at least. Parents may worry about their tomboy, or their son who plays with dolls, but it does not look as if individual children are too bothered, as long as they can keep their parents off their case for a couple of hours.

Loss of parents

But for many young people, something changes at puberty. As sexuality escapes or is released from the deep, it looks around for its old mates – the ones it used to knock around with before it was sent down. In the nuclear family, where the children play in the garden, the object of the happy memories are now hanging, shiftily, around the gates, pretending to be interested in something else, but excited and fearful about who or what is emerging. Surely these harassed and distracted old-timers, waiting without, cannot be the same as those people in the photos, treasured inside, the ones who looked like Tarzan and Jane? We are afraid so. The choice, for the sexual life, is stark but clear. Turn back and batten down, shooting bolts and throwing keys. Or turn away and look elsewhere.

It is the latter course that interests us. For some adolescents, all traces of the parents are treated as suspicious incestuous objects under the skin. Every trait and ethic, doctrine and aspiration, taste and conviction that comes or is felt to come from the parents is a familiar body that beckons and disgusts within. The felt need is to rid, urgently, the centre of the self of these aspects that can no longer be comfortably identified as one's own. The result, famously where it occurs, is the adolescent void, a sense of emptiness and loss, a mood of mourning and depression.

Peter Blos (1962) called adolescence the time of *second* individuation, a stage of radical overhaul of personal identity. Before new lovers can take the place of the relinquished mother and father, there is a period of impoverishment that is the consequence of the distancing from the real parents and estrangement from their inner representations. To fill the gap, a close and special friend may be appreciated for qualities which are similar to those of one of the parents, often the parent of the same sex. This friendship may take on a sudden passionate and obsessive quality. If greater measures are felt to be needed, crushes on older teenagers or adults may develop:

Mary

> Mary overheard her favourite teacher at school telling a colleague she was going to see a film that evening. The film title sounded French. Mary spent over an hour on the telephone trying to find out from local cinemas if they were showing a foreign film that day. She established that a town nearby was holding a film festival, and persuaded her thrilled but bewildered mother to drive her over to see what film was playing. They arrived in time to see Mary's teacher standing in a queue outside the cinema, laughing and holding hands with a man.
>
> 'I couldn't breathe, let alone move or speak. My mother jumped out of the car, unable to contain her excitement at my new-found interest in serious films. I was bolted to the seat in jealous paralysis. The strange thing was, as I finally stumbled out of the car, I realized

that I was not sure who I was more jealous of, my teacher or her boyfriend. I would have happily changed places with either, wishing only to be looked after by the other. In the film that I watched for the next two hours, I was alternately saved from fainting or drowning by a young man or woman, each of whom, singly, took me to their home and nursed back me to full recovery.'

Harvey Greenberg (1975) wrote how the idealization of a hero can offer even greater scope for the healing of narcissistic injury – suffered through loss of the previously worshipped internal parents – and the participation by proxy in another's magnificence:

> Mass media are impressive progenitors of current adolescent heroes. (We think here of stars of popular music, soaps and sports.) The essence of the relationship between teenager and hero is amusingly captured in many of the comic strips that still appeal to adolescents of all ages. Recall how frequently the Superhero has had a teenage sidekick who accompanies the mighty one on his perilous adventures, shares in his miraculous powers – but only to a limited degree – and is constantly rescued from one masochistically tinged predicament after another. The sidekick is likely to live in ambiguous dependency upon the Hero in everyday life. Thus Robin . . . is Batman's . . . *ward*. In another popular strip the omnipotent hero and his charge are condensed when Billy Batson, a crippled [sic] newsboy, is transformed into the valorous Captain Marvel by speaking the magic word, 'Shazam!'

In other flights from awareness of this period of painful 'bereavement', young people may try out many new identities in rapid succession. Or they may, through the exertion and pain of their bodies or the explosive release of their emotions, forcefully ensure an exaggerated experience of personal self, powerful in its centre and certain of its edges. Or, like Sally, they may feel themselves to be most alive and real when they turn their attention inwards and explore their internal world.

Sally's sense of self is intermittent; or, put another way, she allows herself to imagine that her selves are transitional. She feels she is trying to effect a change from living in her parents' version of her to finding her own way with other people. Her diary helps her to verbalize, and thus define, vague ideas about herself. Through her daily writing she externalizes her inner drama and is then able to watch from a few rows back. Moreover, the continuity of the diary helps bind her tentative self together as she can review from time to time her recorded experiences. Does she know what she thinks and what she believes, what she is attracted to and wants? Of course not. So she plays with it all to see how it feels, to see what it is like.

Gary

Gary bothers me more. The kind of man who says he never had an adolescence is just the sort of person who probably invented adolescence in the first place. When I asked him once if he had ever kept a diary, he looked at me as if I had made an improper suggestion. It is not that Gary would worry about his secrets being discovered by somebody else. It is worse than that. He would never get as far as fearing his diary might be read, because it would be too secret even to write!

Gary has an interesting problem that causes him a great deal of inconvenience in his life as a professional person. He is frightened to carry, in his pockets or briefcase, any documentation that contains his name or address. His driving licence, credit cards, passport and other such essential items of modern life are hidden in various and different places in his flat. He leaves home with only the cash he thinks he will need for that day. 'If I collapsed in the street, nobody would know who the hell I was!'

Gary allows me to believe for a few weeks that this is just a rather extreme version of a fear of being mugged and losing money. Then, one day, he blurts out the truth. 'It is ridiculous, of course, but I am terrified that somebody will take something with my name on it and pretend to be me.' I ask him what sort of things he imagines this person might do when pretending to be him. He affects a sort of 'never-really-considered-it' kind of gesture, followed by an 'it-isn't-really-the-point' type of shrug. But I've got his number and sit tight.

I expect a long wait, which turns out to be the case, and to pass the time I bet with myself that the first two or three things he says will be fairly desultory attempts to lose my interest, but by number four if I can last that long, the place should be really jumping. In the event, I lose and he dives straight in. 'Have sex with loads of women; get roaring drunk in pubs and start fights, throwing chairs and tables over; run up huge bills and not pay them; knock the helmets off policemen and sprint off down the backstreets; smash car windows – you know, that kind of thing.'

I feel a bit sheepish now. It is always like that when someone shares a personal fantasy. You don't know where to look. I am surprised it has never occurred to Gary, however, that this fear of having his identity stolen by a stranger is really a fear of being taken over by a strange part of himself. He is astonished when I suggest it. 'I started feeling this way when I was about nine or ten', he says, as if that were some kind of refutation or excuse. 'My mother could never understand how the name tags she sewed on my clothes kept coming off. The reason was that I used to undo the stitching during lessons. I was really compliant at home and school. I never had detentions, always gave work in on time. But I was always frightened of being in trouble.' Of course he was. Obedience is the most extreme form of defiance. Chosen servitude mocks the tyrant's heart, in making a gift of what the dictator needs to believe is already his.

But Gary had other retributions to worry about as well. The picture of his youth was not quite as he first described it. He used to lie. 'Not over important matters, that was the funny thing. I would lie when asked something that nobody could ever check, and where the truth or falsity was of little consequence. Like whether I had seen a television programme, or if I liked a particular song.'

Now he comes to mention it, I realize that I am myself sometimes unsure whether Gary is telling *me* the truth or not. There is never anything I can put my finger on, so to speak, but I have at moments a suspicion that he is stringing me along. I suppose I had entertained previously a vague hypothesis that he had as a child felt lied to rather a lot and was showing me what it was like not to know if people were being straight. But now I have other ideas.

Gary lies to find out whether other people are mindreaders, and whether therefore they know his guilty secrets. He evades the condemnation of his conscience by lying about things that are not important. It is only a game, after all, and play can attract no moral disapproval to itself. But the body, as Freud said, cannot lie. Wait long enough and it will eventually join in the conversation, perhaps in the form of a symptom.

Gary is always rubbing his nose. When somebody looks at him, as I look at him now, it is his immediate gesture of response. It is the cause for him of much distress, mainly because of its involuntary nature. He really cannot stop doing it. Similarly, if anybody sits next to him on a train or bus, he is compelled to put his hands together in front of him, adopting the posture of prayer.

Compulsive acts, in our own law, are inadmissible confessions. They tell other people what we really want to do or think we have already done. That may be good enough, usually, for the thought police to make an arrest, but the judge takes a little more fooling. Gary's solution is to project his conscience on to me; I am mother and father writ large. I can accuse him of no hidden sexual life because his hand is on his nose. It is, therefore, not touching his genitals. At the same time, because his nose stands as it were, for his penis, he masturbates in my face.

I make a similar inference about his behaviour on public transport. There must be a wish to touch the person who sits next to him – to fondle or caress, perhaps to rob. But since his hands are together and in front of him, for all to see, nothing has happened and nothing could. His submissive gesture is evidence to the highest authority of his continuing good intentions and behaviour.

The problem is, these inferences and interpretations, bread and butter though they may be, are all mine. I am a little in awe of Gary's capacity to split and deny, but there is no disputing his suffering. He does feel he is missing out. Why can't he give himself a break?

Alfred Adler apparently used to ask his patients what they would do if they were cured, believing that in his answer to this question the neurotic would give away the nature of the situation he was seeking to avoid. When I ask Gary, his answer is immediate. 'I would be an adolescent.' He wants, as he said, to be found lying in the street. He wants nobody to know who he is. He wants to be free of the restraints, restrictions and magical determinism of his name, the straitjacket of his identity. He thinks you only get this chance once, and he has missed it.

But we can understand Gary's search in a different way, and it has as much to do with the whole of life as with a passing phase. Gary's fear of losing his name through theft is a disguised wish to give it up. Words are magical, names even more so. When we learn the name of somebody or something, we gain power. When we call a person's name, she comes. When we name an object, it is brought to us. But two basic ambiguities are invested in the proper name, those of sex and love. A name is the mark of sexual as well as personal identity. A person's wish to *change* their name may therefore express a wish to be of the opposite sex.

The proper name is also the site of another significant ambivalence. We discover that our name can be used as an endearment or to underscore a scolding. It can be used lovingly or angrily. The same name will, then, have opposite meanings, depending on the tone of voice.

Gary's project may contain these aspects, but seems to circle something that is even more fundamental. It is an unconscious fantasy of rebirth, with the wish, this time around, to be a foundling, lying in the street. He wants to arrive with no name, without, therefore, the commitment to a gender that is assigned to him, and without the confinement to all such fixed positions in the chain of signification, cultural meanings and parental expectations that lay in wait, ready to seize and pin him down, twenty-five years before. Gary is an old-style hero, of ancient mythology and black-and-white television; a man with mission and dream. But he tells his story in the fashion of this age, and, since this is the one I live in, I feel entitled to a modern interpretation as well.

We could trace Gary's attempts to lose his name to a persisting doubt in his origins, itself the disguised fulfilment of an envious desire. If he has no name, he is not his parents' child. They could not have produced him. They could, therefore, have had no creative and sexual relationship of which he need feel jealous, from which he need feel excluded. The difficulty for Gary, however, is that in not allowing his parents to come together internally, he denies the possibility of a link between them that leads to something new: a meeting of minds, as well as bodies, that allows the coming together of different thoughts that can produce new ideas. For himself, the consequent impoverishment is of deep division within him, as parts of himself remain strangers to each other – the passport and driving licence are hidden in different places in the house. He wants, but is unable, to take himself by surprise.

> I want to tell Gary that he is not lying enough. He must start deceiving people about important things and cut out the trivia, to force the moment to its crisis. I should say that I do not feel completely confident about this approach, and restrict it therefore to private entertainment. I have a suspicion that I might be inviting him to lead the life I dare not lead myself, in order to see how he gets on before I have a try. But I reassure myself, to deal with the guilt, that this is anyway the nature of the psychotherapy relationship. Why would we do it, otherwise? I need not worry. He is way ahead of me: 'I will go to a football match, dressed as a woman, and scatter all my headed notepaper in the crowd. Then I'll get high on drugs, stick my bare bottom out of a taxi window and run off without paying.' That should do the trick. As long as next day he remembers to take back his library books. Gary's joke is a serious statement of commitment to the ownership of all his dreams and pledges, and the decision to recognize the present as the stage for their fulfilment or disappointment. My joke is the same.

It is not, then, adolescence that Gary wants, and certainly not the experience of this time that many young people go through. If some psychoanalysts have been mistaken in maintaining that *Sturm-und-Drang* is an essential and inevitable accompaniment to growing up, this is not to deny that internal and external pressures can combine to cause a great deal of suffering and distress.

Brian

> Brian is desperate for help but cannot say so. His rapid changes of feeling and mood are upsetting for his family, but it is clear they trouble him deeply. He hates, however, my interest and concern,

and mocks the impotence of my approach. He thinks we get nowhere together: 'Can you make me good looking? Can you help me to run fast? Can you stop the kids from taunting me at school and on the bus on the way home? No! So what good are you then? The best thing you can do is leave me alone.'

The fluidity of personality, so idealized by Gary, feels like madness to Brian. He is tantalized by the exciting imagery of television, music and fashion that stimulates but does not permit. His peers seem only to embrace these glossy pictures with delight, but Brian is humiliated by the discrepancy between the world they portray and the one he himself lives in. He feels wooden, self-conscious and 'fat', unable, anyway, to participate. He sees himself at the base of the sexual and sporting hierarchy that struts and parades its stuff at school and in the streets. He 'knows' now he will never be the great footballer he once assumed he would be. He 'knows' he will never be attractive to girls.

Brian had, until thirteen or fourteen, been popular with a small group of friends. At sixteen he is lonely and isolated. He frets and fidgets before me, bouncing his right leg up and down on the ball of his foot, while I imagine his weekend, spent sprawling in front of the television, watching that hero video for the seventh or eighth time. I see him unable to move, except to go to the kitchen to eat; or to his bedroom, probably to masturbate, kick his walls and cry. He wants none of these things, but is driven to indulge them, increasing thereby the desperate helter-skelter, the sense of being swept around in the maelstrom of his own life, then dumped in helpless collapse on the sofa.

I am frightened with him, or for him, I am not sure which. In our meetings I feel close to the edge at which Brian trembles, and it is so bad that I dread the day of the week he comes to see me. Or I wake, sometimes, with an anxiety I cannot locate, until I remember I am due to see him that morning. When I empathized one day with how frightened he must feel, he was on his feet at once, shouting in tearful rage. 'How can I be frightened! I've got an iron bar by my bed. Anybody who burgles me will get it wrapped around their head.'

It is impossible not to take it as a warning to me. Brian is persecuted by my attempts to get in touch, to make contact, which he feels to be breaking and entry. The adult movie 'Reality' may offer nothing except walk-on parts of service or attendance in trivial enterprises. There may be no possibility of meaningful achievement or challenge, of contribution or participation, in worthwhile human projects. More probably, it offers restricted viewing, or standing room only, and at times of the day when everyone else is working.

But 'understanding', the reflection of one's suffering in another's eyes, knows no language and imagery in our culture apart from comforting mothers and crying children, both objects of disparagement and contempt, or sentimental idealization. Brian feels I infantilize him with my fellow feeling. He hates me for the tears he chokes back. He feels I try to seduce him back into a universe of safety he longs for but which offends the one-track version of young manhood which is his reality, that world of fierce independence and stoic denial of pain and emotion. It seems to me, however, that Brian would like to smash his own head in, to stop these thoughts, whatever they are, from hurtling into and around his mind.

Evenings are murder in the home. Brian provokes fierce rows with his family. Often these will end in a fight with his younger brother or in Brian's physical restraint by his father. The parents are worried rather than angry about this. They agree with me that Brian tries to have his nightmares before he goes to bed. He certainly settles better after a huge explosion. On other nights they hear him wandering around in the early hours, unable to sleep. Then, in the mornings, he cannot get up.

We struggle to find ways into and out of the vicious cycle. Desolate and forsaken, Brian comfort eats and masturbates, and then condemns himself for his 'weakness'. There is nothing wrong with masturbation, when, as Woody Allen said, it really is having sex with someone you love. In Brian's case, however, it is part of a campaign of self-and-other hate; an envious, spoiling attack on the sexuality of others, a mocking punishment beating of himself. 'Wanker' is a term of real abuse in our culture. Its synonyms are 'fool' and 'idiot', but the incompetence attributed is, of course, sexual. It is a word that sneers at the loneliness of childhood and sees the child's dreams as pathetic. It is spoken, in smug triumph, from the post-coital bed of the adult heterosexual couple; or heard that way, by the excluded child. As Brian feels awful, he repeats the futile attempt at self-gratification, fuelled further, this time, by hopeless resignation. 'Since I am so bad, it no longer matters what I do. I am fat, so I may as well eat. I am no good. I deserve no better.'

It is a problem that surfaces in Brian's adolescence but its origins and causes reach back into his past. Since our children are obliged to be happy, they rightly conclude we cannot tolerate their disappointment. We feel their unhappiness to be an indictment of us, and are compelled either not to see it or to cajole them out of it, leaving them, alone, to bear the responsibility or guilt for the thing that has gone wrong, the catastrophe that is never named.

The gap between aspiration and achievement is the stuff of tragedy, but only on stage and paper. Our own children must not know of failure, and failure, therefore, is all that they know. Apart from moral lectures that nobody ever listens to, they see no evidence of adult commitment to the meaning of suffering and its potential value and resolution. They are distracted from the experience of sharing their distress by the prohibition on its expression, and they have few models of adults who have the courage to acknowledge their own difficulties, and their own faltering attempts at accomplishing personal goals. They do not see us cry like we mean it, without blame and accusation, or without drunken excess. Nor do they see us seek and use peer support. The consequence is, that they are left exposed to the latest mindless hero fantasy, dreamed up by those gangs whose idea of success is the accumulation of wealth, and whose standard of explosive, emotional release, is the firing of a gun.

3
Identity

One in favour, one against and one to play

Our bodies may be only one of the places where we live. Perhaps we have moved out, or not even taken the keys in the first place. Our selves are symbolic and not only corporeal. We are where we believe ourselves to be and can symbolically locate ourselves, wherever we feel a part of us exists or belongs – it may be in our work or our home, our nation or religion. It may be in our gang or football team. It may be in our children.

Susan

Susan, at seventeen, is too much. She suffers, she says in a letter of self-referral, from an excess of subjectivity. When we meet, her head is slightly bowed, her hair drawn like a curtain across her face. Suddenly her head jerks back, the hair is parted, and she shoots me a look of pleading sadness. She motions to shake my hand, and at the same time her right leg strides out to the side, knee bent and foot pointing away at a ninety-degree angle to her left leg. She is embarrassed at what she clearly feels to be this involuntary action. It occurs to me that one half of her is obeying some hidden instruction to turn and run, but the other half is staying put.

She begins with her parents. They had waited a long time to have children (Susan is the elder of two and has a younger brother) because they had wanted everything to be exactly right. They are both very talented people who work, however, in mediocre jobs because they value the security of being able to save for their children's futures. Neither had any higher education, as they came from similar backgrounds where the expectation was that young people would begin work on leaving school. Everybody likes her parents, but people say her mother is very anxious. Her father worries a great deal as well, but manages to hide this, at least from those outside the family. Susan falls silent and appears to be staring at something on the carpet.

I am struck by the fact that she has said nothing about herself, and appears to have no intention to do so as the silence has continued for some time. When I point this out to her she is surprised. She had thought, in her state of self-absorption, that she had been talking. She hastily assembles an account of herself which is delivered without enthusiasm or interest, as though either to please me, or at least, to stop me from bothering her.

She tells me that she is considered very bright at school but cares little for academic success. Others say she is attractive and popular, but she seldom goes out with friends. She appreciates the interest others have in her, and dutifully accepts invitations when they arrive, but feels always on the edge of the group, self-conscious and shy.

We meet on a weekly basis, and Susan is always thoughtful and introspective. There are long gaps between my questions or comments and her responses, and so I often seem to have a lot of time on my hands without being too sure what to do with it. Occasionally in these pauses I am reminded of Field Marshal von Moltke, who was said to be capable of silence in six languages. When some people do not speak very much there can be a powerful evocation of interiority and depth, as though they are carefully considering and assessing an almost infinite number of brilliant and authentic thoughts and ideas.

When I mention her silences to her, Susan confesses to being worried about what I will think of what she says. Her inner play has consisted, she says, of presenting and dismissing a variety of possible things to say: 'I have to censor. It may sound stupid or mad otherwise.'

Since I often feel hurt by her silences, I ask her if she is ever worried about sounding mean or nasty. She looks at me suspiciously as though fearing a trap. There is another long silence. I am on the edge of my chair. Finally comes the word of admission, 'Yes.' I am expecting to need to ask more questions, but she is already elaborating. 'I feel so cross when I am around people. I don't understand why, but I am frightened this anger will just burst out of me if I don't supervise it closely.' She is clear that she does not want to think carefully before she speaks, as though it were a kind of translation exercise. She wants to think as she speaks, or better still, to discover what she thinks as she says things to other people and listens to their responses.

This is helpful and clarifies some of the feelings I struggle with when meeting Susan. I often feel left out. She keeps me hanging on. There is something we should share that she jealously guards to herself – the role of the one who listens, reflects back, joins in and calls forth; the one who is excited, surprised, unsure or angry. It is the role of the other. In early childhood, in our society, it is usually the role of the mother as the child plays and engages. Susan's silence is keeping mum. I in the mean time play alone and am, without feedback or response, unsure. I wait and want but do not get; or I am given to but only when the parent is ready, after great deliberation and planning, but without spontaneity or joy.

When I asked her at our first meeting what she was thinking and she was surprised ('Wasn't I just talking?') it was as though we were as one mind, and mummy always knows what she is thinking. But this internal parent is too attentive and watches her every move. Susan is always centre-stage and in the limelight, and is thus acutely conscious of herself. This self-consciousness solves one problem – it is continuing evidence that she is never on her own, never unseen or unnoticed, her parents are always watching – but creates another. She is never off stage and can therefore never stop performing for the directors. The edge of the group seems the only safe haven. She can be temporarily between acts and protect the audience from her rage at their incessant demands. Unfortunately, it is in darkness there, and, without the script, she is, like me in her silences, unsure what to do or be.

Susan is sobbing convulsively now. She tells me I will despise her and think she is awful when I find out what she is feeling. If I could speak I would reassure her, even though I know I shouldn't, but I am choking myself and nothing is coming out. Her distress is powerfully involving. I have the sense of a sadness that is too much for a parent to see and hear. I am the father who wants only his child's happiness and cannot bear his daughter's pain. She gathers herself to continue. 'I feel so ungrateful. When mum and dad look at me, I don't know who or what they see. It just doesn't feel like me. They have given me so much, all the things they never had themselves. The trouble is that I don't know if I want it all. I don't seem to value anything. I don't know what I want.'

Susan's mother and father cannot allow her to discover her own desire. She is their project. It is paradoxically the case that despite all of the undoubted sacrifice and devotion, it is the daughter who looks after the parents, or, at least, some treasured possessions of theirs – their excited hopes, their dreaming selves. It is she who is always available to them, offering herself, or allowing herself to be used, as the raw material for their creative invention. Susan is the empty space, or place of reception, that feels obliged to offer sanctuary to her parents' unlived conceits, kept for many years in cold storage. They have nothing for themselves apart from her, because she has all that they really want. They have come to stay, but see around them only the gifts or possessions they have themselves brought along.

As Susan's internal parents do not try to get to know her, she remains a stranger to herself. She feels compelled to live out her parents' aspirations; but, angry that they have outstayed their welcome, and unable to ask them to leave, she needs also to refuse to do so. She hopes they will notice, and graciously withdraw. She is lonely and wants to be alone.

Susan looks up and tries to smile. 'I am sorry,' she says. 'You probably don't know what I am talking about.' I am struck that on this first occasion of her expression of ambivalence in regard to her parents she is more aware that she needs to let me know clearly what she is thinking in order to be understood, although ironically I think I was following it anyway. Perhaps the release of anger facilitated an experience of greater separation and differentiation.

She is talking now about how her identity seems insubstantial. She does not feel like a young woman. She feels she has no gender, or rather, no sex. She tells me that her mother refers to her genitals as 'down there'. Her parents can talk about her brother's penis in terms of its practical function of micturition but not as a sexual organ of pleasure. Her clitoris, therefore, was not named.

I ask her how she feels about her parents' relationship with each other. She looks at me suspiciously as though I am inviting her to criticize them, but recognizes it is her own criticism that troubles her. She speaks grandly of a platonic friendship. Somewhere in the account, however, perhaps in her descriptions of their attitudes to pleasure, I catch the sense of self-and-other denial.

I am reminded that Susan has been ill for some time and has seen several doctors. I wonder whether this might not be a good sign. Perhaps her body is insisting on some recognition of its universe and is protesting about the world of symbols in which Susan seems hopelessly trapped, exclusively submerged. But it is more of the same. The illness is formless, unclear, ill-defined and contested. Does it really exist? Is there such a thing? The contempt Susan claims to hear in the doctors' talk of a 'psychosomatic condition' mirrors her contempt for her self. It is a sham and has no demonstrable shape or force.

Infant observation and research studies confirm that the psyche of the newborn is no blank screen. From the earliest days the baby is captivated by the voices of its carers, follows objects with its eyes, and engages in bodily, facial and vocal movements and expressions that are its opening gestures of relationship. We are a gregarious and sociable species. Community is primary and social properties are inherent in the human animal. The individual and the isolate are products of society.

One of the central tenets of psychoanalytic theory is that all modes of relating to others will invariably change throughout a person's life. However, even the most primitive feelings about oneself and others that derive from the earliest states of mind in the first relationships will remain as a permanent backdrop to experience, potentially disrupting or overwhelming more rational assessments of what we think is happening between us.

Stephen

Stephen is seven. From very early in his life his parents used to put him into care on a regular basis because they could not cope. When he was six he was again fostered at the request of his mother, who complained that he was throwing his faeces in the house. He was looked after by an elderly and very experienced foster-couple. Every evening Stephen enjoyed the routine of being read to as he prepared for sleep. One night he came into the bedroom of his foster parents and stood at the foot of their bed. The foster father woke to see Stephen staring at him. He thought Stephen must be sleep-walking and got up to help him back to bed. Stephen spoke: 'Uncle, can I tell you a story?'

It was to be the beginning of a series of accounts Stephen would give about his life with his birth parents. The narrative was confused and confusing, with no recognizable sequences and time scales, but the theme was clear. Stephen had been subjected to appalling and humiliating experiences of sexual and physical abuse by his parents and their friends. He had been made to act out with adults scenes from pornographic films they would watch together, and had been directed to have sex with his younger brothers and sisters.

I met Stephen with his foster-father, a kind and caring man who had firm and traditional ideas about raising children (he was himself a grandfather), but someone who had a clear sense of fun. Stephen raced past me into my room and grabbed the nearest box of toys – it happened to be Lego – and began sticking pieces together. He had his back to me, but I had caught a glimpse of him as he had darted past me and I had the fleeting impression of a child who looked like a small animal, perhaps some kind of rodent.

The foster father began to speak to me as Stephen sat on the floor between us. I noticed he would either speak of Stephen as if he were not there, or as if he could not possibly understand what was being said even if he were there. The tone of the discourse was harsh and punitive, a string of complaints or tales of what Stephen had done wrong during the previous week. After some minutes of this, the foster-father would occasionally ask Stephen to confirm one of his misdemeanours. 'Tell Paul what you did yesterday.' Stephen's reponse would always be to give one word, the name of the offence: 'Stealing.' He would show no other reaction and would then continue to stick and unstick the Lego pieces.

I was surprised at the foster-father's manner as it was in such marked contrast to the man I had seen two days previously when we had met without Stephen to discuss psychotherapy. Before the foster-father left us, I tried to engage Stephen in some conversation. He did not acknowledge that I had spoken. 'This is Stephen,' said the foster-father as he was leaving, 'he just plays.' If only he did; if only he could.

Stephen tired quickly of the Lego and searched frantically and voraciously around the room, trying every door and cupboard and scattering the contents of boxes onto the floor. He found a game, continually changed the rules, and then alternated between talk of 'thrashing' me and then sweetly trying to help me. Clearly he thought that the rules were always against him, and that people made them up and broke them when they pleased. 'I like games. I play with anybody.' It felt very promiscuous. 'Uncle doesn't like games.'

I had worried that the foster-father ('Uncle') had locked into something very punitive, but it was apparent that this was something Stephen powerfully recreated. I found myself irritated at times, especially with his clumsy insistence that he do and take things for himself. I felt as though I wanted to enact a kind of training relationship with him, as one might with an animal. I wanted to bark: 'Do this! Don't do that! Sit down!' There seemed no point in speaking to him. This very little boy scurried around the room and under my feet and I thought, without humour, that anything I said would go over his head. Such interactions as we had were about being lead astray or tricked. Usually he would try to mislead me. Once he accused me of tricking him, only to say that my tricks were no good.

Stephen would continually ask me what the time was and how much longer we had left, but appeared to gain little from my answers. Suddenly, out of the blue, he wolf-whistled. The closest to sustained play took place when Stephen discovered the hospital play kit. 'I've been doctored,' he announced. He tried to examine me, and I suggested he use one of the dolls he had previously coveted. 'I don't like them,' he said, displacing, perhaps, the feeling that he had been rejected by me. He knocked over a box and blamed me. I tried to empathize about feeling blamed all the time when he didn't know what he had done wrong. 'You chatter too much,' he said.

He wanted to play draughts. 'The big ones (kings) can take the little ones, but the little ones can't take the big ones,' he told me. He picked up the draught pieces and threw them at me. 'You clumsy idiot,' he shouted.

He climbed on top of a chest of drawers, asked me if it was safe, and then violently threw down at me everything that was up there. He ordered me in a contemptuous and controlling voice to draw him a bunny rabbit. He then said he would draw it himself, and told me to close my eyes. I said I would not do this, thinking of his feeling that people had closed their eyes for so long to what had happened to him. He made a card and told me he was taking it home because I was selfish. Did I know the police number? If I did not, then I could not phone them. If I did not let him take something home he was going to jump out of the window and never visit me again. He then told me I was his best friend.

It was close to the end of our meeting and I let Stephen know how many minutes remained. He decided to have a puppet show in which all the animals died immediately. I tried to talk about how sad this was, this awful mess – who can we trust? who can we turn to? who can we believe, when people say they like us and treat us so badly? I was about to relate the deaths in his puppet show to the feelings aroused by my talking about the end of our time, when Stephen cut across me. 'It's only sad because you are talking. Next time there will be no talking.' He grabbed something from the room and fled out of the door, hurtling towards the waiting-room. I found him sitting on his foster-father's lap. He would not look at me or say good-bye. I was not there.

Naming and being named

The playful chatter of babies and carers is already conversation. The word 'infant' means without speech, but in one sense there is no infancy. The baby babbles and patters as its contribution to the first spoken dialogues. Such evolving patterns of understanding and meaning can become lively shared language when parents and their young are together for long periods and where the parties are sensitive to each others' feelings and needs.

Where this is not the case, as with Stephen, the speech is broken. It is broken because the spontaneous movement towards others meets no welcoming response of recognition and the baby gives up. Or the lively, desiring and demanding baby is shouted down by the louder voices of the big kings and queens, who 'can take the little ones when the little ones cannot take them'. When speech starts up again, it is in the form of imperative assaults and stabs. The words are hard (concrete) objects that are thrown by one person at another.

When we describe the birth and development of the self we speak of psychological structures like the ego that cannot, of course, be seen but whose effects or absence are apparent. Stephen struggles to maintain some autonomy in terms of the deluge of perceptions and feelings that swarm over and engulf him. He is hurled and swirls around in a chaos of rapidly shifting visual images and sensations to which he can only helplessly react, lacking much of a capacity to bring order to this confusion, by separation, distinction and classification. He has little ability to hold back, to check his responses or entertain alternative plans or possible solutions among which he can then choose. He is compelled to keep moving. He is on the run. Stephen has no sense of time because he has no secure anchor points. For him there is no past and future. He lives, like the 'frozen' children described by psychotherapist Mrs Dockar Drysdale (1993), in a continuous present, where he is always vulnerable to memories and sensations that feel to him like they are real events in the moment, that he experiences them. He is without barrier and buffer. He has no skin. If with me he is reminded of experiences of being seduced and tricked, blamed and betrayed, bullied and tantalized, then this is what he thinks I am actually doing to him, and he must run or defend himself as best he can.

Naming and symbolizing

Stephen lacks a symbolic attitude. He has no fixed position of internal reference, no socially designated and personally claimed symbol of subjectivity and agency that could facilitate his attempts to detach himself from the infinite complexity of the perceptual universe. To a large extent such essential inner furniture is constructed from language, from being named by others, and then in turn from learning the names of the people and things in the immediate environment (Rumpelstiltskin understood this – name it and nail it). In this way persons and objects can be defined as distinct and distinguishable from each other, and can then be assigned a value. Such linguistic symbols are evidence of, and help to maintain, a distance between ourselves and our immediate internal and external experience.

Our capacity to symbolize provides some cushioning protection from catastrophic reaction to stimulation, but there is more. Our entire personalities are in fact largely our habits of speech. We are whatever we think we could say. Each young child, as it learns to speak, refers to itself first at 'me' and then only secondarily as 'I'. The child thinks of himself as an object of others before he can become an active subject. He can become aware of his own feelings and those of others only by taking the attitude of the other person towards himself and identifying with their perception. Whatever feeling states he may have – of hunger, cold, terror or tiredness – will remain, in Winnicott's words, as 'external as a clap of thunder' until he can unite his perceptions with the empathic perception of someone else. The child can only get to know himself by being known by someone else.

It is not the case that Stephen's difficulties are the simple consequence of his abuse, sexual and emotional. These abuses are themselves the consequences of a prior underlying problem where Stephen's parents were unable to recognize from the outset his emerging subjectivity and treated him mainly as an object whose function was to meet their needs – they could not facilitate his move from 'me' to 'I' – or to become the receptacle for their own uncontained excesses. In most other respects he was ignored; when he was not there to be or do something for them, he was not there at all.

Stephen does not know about sadness, and seems not to have the capacity to feel any emotions. How could he? He is right when he says 'It is only sad because I talk'. The child, as William James pointed out, does not cry because he is sad. It is the other way around: the child is sad because he cries; he is happy because he smiles. When we smile or cry and are in the presence of those who can see us as separate centres of feeling states and initiative, there are consequences and responses. In this way we learn the full meaning of our feelings and actions from the empathic response of those around us. We have the chance to perceive and know ourselves to be sad and happy. We construct an emotional vocabulary and live an emotional life by registering the impact and effects of our actions, after we carry them out. The consequences of our behaviour are recorded in the form of the personal style of our carers. When Stephen cries, there is no concerned response, so he does not feel sad. He continues to parent himself in the same way and blanks out or fails to recognize his own burgeoning feeling states. He recreates his early relationships by inducing others to punish, abuse or ignore him; or he exploits, uses and seduces.

Stephen has little sense of being an autonomous 'I'. He has remained, rather, what Maud Mannoni the French psychoanalyst called 'a me-in-the-eyes-of-another' (1973). This is because the traumas he was subjected to happened before he could represent himself symbolically, before he could speak for himself. They remain, then, not in the form of memories that can be repressed or retrieved, but are unassimilated and unprocessed sensation states, whose only form of expression is in acting out.

These two young people illustrate in contrasting ways the obstacles and dangers that lie in the path of the self as it struggles for an individual and independent life that is compatible with close relationships with others. We all begin our lives totally dependent on somebody else to recognize, and then realize, our needs and wishes. Without this experience, we have no chance to know and become ourselves. As the sociologist Franklin Giddins said, it is not that two heads are better than one; it is that two heads are needed for one. This means we are extremely vulnerable to both a lack of interested response and to intrusion.

We know that babies are born to relate and seek relatedness. Our best practice is where we recognize and get to know each baby as a person in her own right, with her own thoughts, her own feelings and her own ways of expressing herself. She has special things to say that distinguish her from everyone else, but also join her to them. We listen to her and remember what she says. We speak to her. As she expresses herself she gets to know herself as her contributions and gestures are received and reflected back. We do this because this is what we want.

We facilitate, further, the possibility of symbolic representation of self and others and entry into human culture by allowing, without retaliation, the baby's angry attacks of frustration and hate. When the consequences of rage are not felt to be the destruction of all that is relied upon and safe, anger can be acknowledged and its origins and causes recognized. When attacks are survived and care continues, separation and difference can be tolerated and a representational life of symbols is possible. Part of the growth of an individual will be the acquisition and development of a set of personal symbols for that which is loved and lost, and recognized not to be under omnipotent control.

Gender matters

Babies are born into cultures where the potentially infinite number of ways in which experience could be organized is already delimited, already fixed into predetermined meanings, into which the emerging subject is inserted. Language casts its net: what can and cannot be said has already been decided. Nowhere is this more true than in regard to gender. At the moment of birth we are, in other people's eyes, our genitals. Later we will become what we do with them. We will be homosexual or heterosexual. The very first thing the baby notices is that, in terms of speech, he is spoken about and imprisoned by definition rather than addressed directly. He will hear: 'It's a boy! (Does he take sugar?)' rather than, 'Hello! Welcome! We look forward to getting to know you and your getting to know us, a process that will take us all our lives.'

Freud imagined a visitor from another planet who would be struck by nothing so forcibly as 'the fact of the existence of two sexes among human beings'. He also was of the view that this division was of no great consequence to little children who were, until the Oedipus Complex, undifferentiated in terms of psychosexuality. Somewhere between the ages of three and six years old, however, subjectivity and gender identity cohere. All children take up the position of male or female, even though there may be no exact correspondence with biology and physiology; even though they may feel neither certain nor confident that they are in the right camp.

To imagine or remember oneself as of the other gender, or in a predifferentiated bisexual state, is, by this argument, impossible after this time. Imagination and memory are influenced and determined by the position to which one has been assigned and the specific and discrepant mental categories for the organization of perception and experience, which are the consequences of this particular paradigm of opposition.

Perhaps we do not try hard enough. Perhaps it is not the kind of issue that is soluble by thinking alone, to the consternation and disappointment of the over-developed solitary and verbal aspects of ourselves. We may need to do something; worse still, we may need to feel something and share our feelings with other people.

The argument has become entangled with contemporary notions of desire, the modern way to celebrate the impossible. Freud once said that 'we must reckon with the possibility that something in the nature of the sexual instinct itself is unfavourable to the realization of complete satisfaction.' Lacan (1966) developed this idea to say that we only long for others or objects when they have become lost to us through awareness of absence or lack. Any satisfaction we subsequently achieve, therefore, will always be permeated by this sense of loss. But the standard of satisfaction implied by this argument is of something not worth aspiring to anyway. It sounds like 'fulfilment', or what the novelist Joyce Carol Oates called the unerotic pleasure of having it all over and done with.

Awareness of loss, absence and lack make excitement, interest and movement possible, even if painful sometimes. It may be that what is revealed in those other ideas, is an unconscious fantasy that pain and suffering cannot be borne and recovered from. But pain itself – whether of jealousy, disappointment, longing or rage – is an intense feeling state that must therefore be central to and serve to sustain all other high-excitement states, including pleasure and love. It seems unlikely that we could anaesthetize or tone down suffering and still be happy.

The idea of language as irrevocably determinative requires a similar qualification. It is true that we inherit and learn a code, the use of which restricts our freedom, because meanings are predetermined. But we are not necessarily and absolutely passive in regard to our response to this language that we stumble into. If a child is raised in a non-impinging environment, where the fact and individual pace of her spontaneous generation of wishes and needs is respected and responded to, she will grow with a core belief in her capacity to make an impact on her surroundings, to influence and change others and elicit the response she seeks. She will believe in the magical power of her words and she will be right. She will adapt and change the code, in the humour and poetry of ordinary speech. She will create history – not, as Marx said, just as she pleases (often it will be just as she does *not* please) – but in dialogue with (and on the shoulders of) present and previous generations.

Robert

Robert, at seventeen, has solved the problems of sexual identity for himself. He wants surgery to become a woman. He has felt 'trapped' in the wrong body for as long as he can remember. At the ages of five, six and seven, he liked to play with girls' toys and wear the clothes of his sisters and their friends.

He is tolerant, charmed even, by my attempts to interpret his wish and regard it as a psychological manner, or an issue of cultural stereotyping. I find myself irritated and needing to argue. I feel officious and am looking to score points. I am unsure whether this is pure counter-transference and I am caught up in the recreation of a past relationship of Robert's, or whether it is a difficulty of mine that is touched. Probably the price I pay for conforming to the psychological generalizations about being male is greater than I care to admit and I am defensively angry and frightened. I am not the only one who is bothered. The referral letter from the family doctor mentions Robert's maternal grandmother on two occasions when it is clear from other remarks in the correspondence that it was the paternal grandmother who was meant.

Robert often speaks about himself by reporting his mother's comments or observations with pride and satisfaction: 'My mother thinks I am very much like her. She thinks we both feel and suffer a great deal. If she is unsure about what to wear or how to decorate the house she always asks me because she says we have the same taste.'

It is Robert's perception that his relationship with his mother is one of similarities. From his account there is no sense that his mother has ever seen her son as other, as being different in body or mind from herself. If this were true, and not simply the misrepresentations required to sustain Robert's wishful fantasy, it is difficult to see how she could have done her part to promote the development of a psychically separate sense of self in him which requires some differentiation.

Robert's father, in his son's version of him at least, is not much help either. Robert describes his father in the language of caricature. He is exaggeratedly masculine and is scornful of all things feminine. I take this to mean that Robert feels his father to be intolerant of vulnerability and emotion, but he admits to no disappointment in this regard. It is not the failure of his father to offer any worthwhile model of being male that is the problem. Robert just likes girls' things and prefers women. He wants to be made into a woman.

In my combative mood I tell him that this sounds like a disguised form of misogyny. It is as though he is saying that the female-born girl or woman is no longer needed. In the silence that follows I begin to feel rather pathetic. At first I think this is because I should not have made that remark, but I begin to realize that it made no impact anyway. Robert has a disdainful and superior way of treating my contributions or protests as though they were beneath contempt and not worthy of a response. When I remember things he has said, reflect back his thoughts or otherwise confirm or affirm his thoughts or ideas, he smiles pleasantly at me and I feel good. What comes from me as difference meets indifference and promotes a mood of impotent petulance in me.

I have no difficulty empathizing with Robert's existential struggle. It is in a way the reverse. I am at a loss to understand why everybody does not wrestle with the rigid categories of identity and gender. My understanding deserts me, however, in regard to Robert's stubborn insistence in reducing this conflict so crudely to one of the body. How could he actually want to subject himself to such vicious and violent surgery? The only way I can think about it sometimes, is as a desperate attempt to recapture some feeling in a body that has become numb or anaesthetized from repression, as in Wilhelm Reich's ideas about defensive armour. Perhaps pain for Robert would be proof of being alive.

In another moment of uncontained behaviour on my part, I put it to him one day that his 'solution' to his difficulties is no different from that of tall or fat women, who, under pressure from the glossy magazine pictures that determine what attractive females are supposed to look like, have lengths of bone or layers of flesh removed. What did he think about that? Did he feel that black people in a racist society should have their skin colour changed? Or that disabled people should be rebuilt and have 'proper' bodies? He does not, of course, give these provocative attempts to catch him out, the time of day. Okay, I admit it, I lost my rag. But at least I am right!

Robert finds separations unbearable. At the end of each of our meetings he embarks sometimes on long anecdotes delivered in an animated manner that seem impossible to interrupt. At other times he tells me something that worries me greatly in an attempt to keep me thinking about him when he is away. I feel either that I will never get away from him, or that I dare not let him go because I am consumed by an anxiety that some terrible thing will happen to him or me if we part. Sometimes I am enraged. He, however, will not acknowledge that he feels any anger towards me as representing a parent who abandons. He does not recognize the fear of being swamped, taken over or engulfed that he induces in me.

At first I hear Robert's camp mode of speaking as another example of simulation, as in the ways he identifies with the superficial cultural clichés of what constitutes femininity. He has told me how he buys women's clothes, by which he means frilly or

> lace garments, and wears them at home. His idea of what is female is the same as that of the drag queen, with the exaggeration of certain archetypes based on the external or visible. It is about behaviour and social role, limited and restricted in cliché. It is never about other human qualities.
>
> But I realize also that he speaks with a lisp in a way that the early founders of psychoanalysis might have understood as indicating a pre-dental character. Within the metaphor of undifferentiation, it is as though he has not allowed himself to be weaned. He will not use his teeth to bite off and chew, to make something his own by taking apart what he sees or is given. He swallows whole.
>
> Robert believes that anatomy is fate, but not destiny. Destiny, like destination, is the end-station, the place that is reached. He believes he can choose where to go. He is right, of course, but in one sense he is more possessed by his body than I am by mine. He maintains that who he feels himself to be, is absolutely determined by the body he happens to be born with (fate), and the body he wants, through surgery, to have constructed (destiny).

It is, of course, true that selfhood is predicated on the body. We are embodied selves and the development of personhood presupposes bodily experience and the mental elaboration of body processes and events. But the self is not exhausted when the body collapses into its organs and surfaces.

Freud believed that anatomical difference was the bedrock, the point beyond which psychoanalysis could not go. He believed, famously, that a woman cannot give up her wish for a penis. (Ferenczi (1989) maintained that the reason the penis was so valued by both sexes was that its ownership guaranteed reunion with the mother through copulation with a woman who could later represent her. Castration would then mean vulnerability to the primitive terrors of separation anxiety.) He also believed that a man cannot conquer his fear of being in the feminine position.

We have moved on from there, within and without psychoanalysis. It is clear that many people do live parts of their lives with a disregard for the external attributes and activities that supposedly constitute being male or female. Nevertheless, it is apparent that most of us feel our masculinity or femininity, however we understand these terms, to be central to our sense of ourselves.

But the reason for this is no anatomical reflex. A whole set of conscious and unconscious fantasies, about sexual identity and attitudes to the body, are in the minds and behaviour of parents and carers, those local spokespeople for the dominant cultural attitudes. All of these phenomena exercise a determining influence on development, by subtly interacting with whatever the infant brings.

Body image has its roots in the earliest experiences of feeding and care – holding, touching, caressing, smiling, dressing and undressing, soft talking; this is love's play in anybody's language. For mother-raised children, one major factor will be her relationship to her own body as a woman and a mother, and her relationship to those other bodies she has been persuaded are different. Another will be the child's perception of the direction, quality and extent of his parents' or carers' interest in their own peer relationships of love and intimacy.

Sexuality and sexual identity will be constructed on the basis of identifications with the real and imagined aspects of the relationships of the child's carers with each other and with their male and female adult friends within the community in which they live. Where those relationships are perceived as loving and reciprocal, with parity in the capacities and desires of all parties to give and receive pleasure and support from each other, a child will have the opportunity to conclude that either gender is fine and the adult world is worth joining.

A child that lives with both parents can tolerate their relationship when that relationship is felt to be tolerable. Such a relationship will need to have observable qualities of mutual appreciation and enjoyment, with the commitment and ability to resolve conflict. It will need to be desired enough by the couple to be defended from envious attack; safe enough to welcome the interest and contribution of others. This is of critical importance. A child's development depends not only on the capacity to participate in relationships, a necessary condition of which will be good experiences as a participant in the nursing couple. It requires also the capacity to be aware of other relationships in which he or she does not participate. This latter will be influenced greatly by the parents' attempts to recognize, without rejection, the separateness of each other and their children.

Robert's difficulties around separation have inspired a different response. He refuses to acknowledge it. He thinks he can alleviate this, for him, unbearable central anxiety through an enacted unconscious fantasy of symbiotic fusion with his mother. If they can become one and the same by having the same body, then the dangers of separation are eliminated; he can become his mother.

There are other imagined benefits too. Robert can deny the facts of his conception and birth, and create a new female child. He can be his own mother and father. He can deny, renounce and destroy what his parents have made together, motivated perhaps by a furious envy or a judgement that their relationship was not good enough to have produced anything worthwhile. But whatever the motive, this intractable and stubborn fantasy has profound consequences for his identity.

Development depends on the capacity to recognize and acknowl edge that the parental relationship is procreative; that two separate and different people can establish a link between them, that leads to something and somebody new. The child must allow that other bodies and minds can meet and come together for the production of new thoughts and ideas, in order to become able to make connections and think for himself.

Robert is careful to inform me that he experiences no sexual excitement from wearing women's clothes. His attitude suggests he regards such possibilities as perverse. He is trying to tell me why he is no transvestite. The clothes are, then, the symbolic representation of the presexual (or rather pregenital) mother. When he wears them he re-establishes the symbiosis of their earliest days.

Similarly, Robert is contemptuously moralistic in regard to homosexuality. Like his father he hates 'queers'. There was a boy he had known recently with whom he had been in love and they had kissed. Robert, however, had kissed 'as a woman'.

I want to tell him that in my view all men kiss as women. All men are sisters and mothers. Sexuality is always psychosexuality, an amalgam of fantasies interwoven with the stories and characters of our internal dramas. By inclusive combination we become, if we allow ourselves and are allowed by others, all those we have known and loved.

But Robert is angrily and inaccessibly self-contained. He cannot be reached, influenced or changed. He is impenetrable. For me to get through to Robert, I feel I would need to attack him savagely. Such an attack, of course, is what he wants for his body in the form of surgery. He wants parts of himself cut off. He wants holes made in himself through incision. Was it his experience, as a little child, that somebody very important and needed was vain and unreceptive? Is it that person's body he wished to attack and viciously dismember, so that this desired operation is in fact a reparative gesture, an act of atonement through pain, the principle of talion?

Perhaps the operation represents, after all, a tacit acknowledgement of his parents' sexual relationship. The primal scene takes place in the operating theatre. Somebody is being violent, the surgeon/father, and somebody is being hurt, the mother/child. There is also somebody on the outside looking in, uncomprehending and frightened, the child who is me.

The repressed is returning. There is need and reliance in this story. The doctor is a sort of midwife who is necessary for the delivery of this new person. Furthermore, Robert's understanding is that after the operation he will need hormone injections on a regular and long-term basis. This seems to gratify a need for maximal dependence and minimal autonomy. He is clearly pleased at the prospect. He can stay with his mother, as it were, for ever – a slight advance on being fused with her.

4
Compulsive Activity in Adolescence

'Give me chastity and continence, but not yet.'
St Augustine of Hippo

'Please God, lead me into temptation.' Jennie Lee (1980)

The word 'adolescence' comes from Latin and means to blossom and grow. In another language we speak of hormones and the maturation of the sex-specific type. The origin of the word 'sex' lies in Roman Catholic theology, and derives from the Latin word for 'six', the number of the Sixth Commandment of that faith. Adolescence lies between infantile sexuality and adultery. In 1805, before even the unconscious was invented, a printer's error in the Bible actually instructed an astonished and excited readership to have other relationships outside of marriage. 'Thou shalt commit adultery', it intoned. The edition became known as the 'wicked Bible'. Later, Oscar Wilde was to muse sympathetically: 'The chains of marriage are heavy, and it takes two to carry them – sometimes three.'

Adolescents, as we expect, have as much trouble with blossom and growth as the rest of us. Probably more. They have our problems to deal with as well as their own. Peter Wilson and Virginia Bottomley (1978) wrote once that the impact of the adolescent on his or her surroundings during puberty is equivalent to the impact of puberty on the adolescent. We could probably put this the other way round as well. The impact felt by the adolescent of the adults in her or his life is equivalent to the impact of the young person's puberty on them.

In collusive collaboration with our young, we identify adolescence as the time zone in which to dip some digits into fluidity, let it all hang out and not spare the horses. But the order of childhood that is subjected to direct and vicarious attack at this time must be restored in the end (at the latest by midnight on the twenty-fifth birthday). It is needed to reassure, in the past that continues, that we neither kill nor have sex with our families.

Any disturbance of routine represents a breakdown of the parents' law and the breakthrough of forbidden wishes. With timetables to regulate our days and development, we rest assured we will not commit the sins and crimes we entertain. When we know in advance what we will do next, we need have no concern that our excitement may induce us to do the things we are frightened of. Adolescents are followed by adults.

Addiction

Compulsive activity is a caricature of planning and routine. Its enactment is a continuing loyal commitment to those who first trained us – we crack, now, our own whips on ourselves. Where the act that we force ourselves to carry out is absurd or self-injurious, it ridicules or attacks the parents of our childhood. But its present benefit is the protection it offers from the menace of dangerous spontaneity with the attendant threats of murder, incest and the rest of it. We must, indeed, be careful of what we wish for because it may arrive. In the face of this, addiction can seem the solution.

Addiction is an attempt to freeze time and desire. One scenario of need and gratification dominates the waking hours and obliterates other potential interests and concerns. In addiction, we have only one thing on our minds:

> 'Thing is though, Spud,' says Mark Renton to his friend in Irvine Welsh's novel *Trainspotting*, 'whin yir intae skag, that's it. That's aw yuv goat tae worry aboot. Ken Billy, ma brar, likes? He's jist signed up tae go back intae the fucking army. He's gaun tae fuckin' Belfast, the stupid cunt. Ah always knew that the fucker wis tapped. Fuckin' imperialist lackey. Ken whit the daft cunt turned roond 'n sais tae us? He goes: Ah cannae stick civvy street. Bein in the army, it's like bein a junky. The only difference is thit ye dinnae git shot at saw often being a junky. Besides, it's usually you that does the shootin'.
> – That, eh, likesay, seems a bit eh, fucked up, like, man. Ken?
> – Naw but, listen the now. You jist think aboot it. In the army thay dae everything fir they daft cunts. Feed thum, gie the cunts cheap bevvy in scabby camp clubs tae keep thum fae gaun intae toon 'n lowerin' the fuckin' tone, upsettin' the locals 'n that. Whin they git intae civvy street, thuv goat tae dae it aw fir thumsells.
> – Yeah, but likesay, it's different though, cause . . . Spud tries to cut in, but Renton is in full flight. A bottle in the face is the only thing that could shut him up at this point; even then only for a few seconds.
> – Uh, uh . . . wait a minute, mate. Hear us oot. Listen tae whit ah've goat tae say here . . . what the fuck wis ah sayin . . . aye! Right. Whin yir oan junk, aw ye worry aboot is scorin. Oaf the gear, ye worry aboot loads ay things. Nae money, canne git pished. Goat money,

drinkin too much. Cannae git a burd, nae chance ay a ride. Git a burd, too much hassle, cannae breathe withoot her gittin oan yir case. Either that, or ye blow it, and feel aw guilty. Ye worry aboot bills, food, bailiffs, these Jambo Nazi scum beatin us, aw the things that ye couldnae gie a fuck aboot whin yuv goat a real junk habit. Yuv just goat one thing tae worry aboot. The simplicity ay it aw. Ken whit ah mean?'

Heroin is the first word to excite in thinking about adolescents and addiction. All the ingredients of sexuality and violence are waiting in ready association – hard drugs; hard penises; hard men and women. But one of Freud's great discoveries was the way in which phenomena at the extremes throw light on the centre. Everybody, he pointed out, hears voices. This is what it means to have a conscience. It is just that in paranoid states these voices seem to come from further away. In the same way, we are all mad at night, or whenever we dream.

Despite this, it would be an odd use of language to speak of ourselves as addicted to those physical and social activities that we take to be essential – eating, drinking, eliminating, sleeping, or seeking the company of others. Yet these ordinary and everyday experiences are ones we must have, and even in their temporary absence we can become acutely distressed. Perhaps the centre sometimes lights up the dark place where the extremist hides.

Daniel

Daniel is addicted to food. He is eighteen and weighs twenty stone. Every day for the past two years, after a huge breakfast at home, he has carried out a careful ritual at his local café: 'I arrive at 1 pm and leave at 2.30 pm. I have coffee-cake and a milkshake to start, and then order a big meal. Usually it is steak and kidney pie or fried chicken. It comes, on all occasions, with chips and boiled potatoes. I then have a sweet – treakle tart, spotted dick, chocolate sponge and custard – and a coffee to wash it down.'

Daniel sits, always, in his favourite seat by the window, even though this is not without problems. Sometimes passers-by stare through and make him feel uncomfortable. If a bus comes to a halt in traffic outside the café, Daniel puts down his knife and fork and waits until the watching passengers have gone before he resumes eating.

I suggest to him that this aspect of the ceremony of his meal indicates a conflict between guilt (or shame) and triumph or defiance. He has his cake and eats it too. His is self-conscious about his indulgence, and yet determined that others should see what he has on his plate.

Daniel agrees that he feels he is doing something wrong when he eats. He is quiet, but conveys somehow that he is aligning himself with me in the shared task of formulating a hypothesis as to what this guilt may be about. I wait thoughtfully and expectantly. He takes, instead, another course. He tells me that when he leaves the café, he goes to the newsagent next door and buys a bar of chocolate. I feel cheated, let down and full of rage. Daniel had not, after all, used his silence to think with me. He was putting down his knife and fork.

Other strong feelings of mine recur and gather strength in weekly psychotherapy with Daniel. He referred himself to me initially because he was concerned at his addiction to food. I should not be surprised, therefore, that he is obsessed with food and thinks and talks constantly about it. Yet something in his manner continues to trouble me. It is as though he can only operate with a food currency.

I often begin each session with a feeling of great warmth towards Daniel. I look forward to seeing him and remember, fondly, gestures, looks or mannerisms from previous occasions. However, by the end of each session I am left feeling that Daniel sees me only as a potential provider or depriver of food, and that I have neither value nor significance for him apart from this. It is true that the food he seeks from me is in attempt symbolic, and takes the form of advice or reassurance, but the metaphors of my experience with him are dominated by the felt imagery of hoarding or being devoured. He wants me to give him everything, and straight away. I want to keep what I have to myself, for fear I will have nothing left.

Every week, usually around the midpoint of each session, Daniel asks me what I will be doing for him at our next meeting. At a stroke, he manages to communicate his view that he sees our times together in terms of provision, while projecting all responsibility for this provision on to me. Through his flight into the future, he both dismisses and discounts what is presently on offer, and signals his intolerance of gaps. Furthermore, whatever I say to Daniel he asks me to repeat, even though it is clear he had heard me the first time. He always wants double helpings. I, in the meantime, feel I am fighting for my own life.

I hesitate to describe this mood of our time together as a meeting or conversation. I am at these moments instrument and not agent. It is as though any needs, desires or other functions of my own are not recognized. I am no parent, lover or friend of others. I am no thinker of my own thoughts. Worse still, no other human problem, apart from Daniel's addiction, appears worthy of anybody's attention. The world is too little with us.

Christopher Bollas (1987) writes of the infant's inherited potential, encountering after birth the transformational aspect of its mother. The mother is not perceived by the baby as a definite and solid individual person in her own right, but rather as a process, or range of possibilities, that can transform experiences and feeling states for the baby. These may be fundamental physical changes, as from the pangs and pains of hunger to contented satiation, or mental ones, from primitive terrors and agonies to a sense of safety and well-being. It may be the beginnings of the suggestion to the baby of the world of other people through her mirrored responses and chosen gestures.

This aspect of infancy continues for us throughout life and is apparent in certain ways of behaving and relating to other people and things. Sometimes we seek in persons or places, situations or substances, a quality or property that functions to signify transformation. 'The quest is not to possess the object; rather the object is pursued in order to surrender to it as a medium that alters the self,' says Bollas. Being cared for is being changed.

In his longing pursuit, Daniel identifies me solely in terms of my function to change him in some way. Any other network of meaning or relationship that involves me is not recognized. Like the early mother, I am not recognized as Other, but as a needed part of himself.

Daniel lived with his mother until he was two. Since that time he has never seen her again. The photograph he brought me once of mother and son showed a couple very much in love. However, he has heard from his social workers that his mother was prone to depression, and decided one day she could no longer look after him.

The Daniel who has been loved evokes in me a selfless and generous care. But I am also felt to tantalize and withhold. I have much to offer and give, but from his point of view it is I who decide when we meet and when we finish. I set the menu, determine the size of the portions and the speed of service, but he cannot be sure, in my depression, when I am open. I sit by the window flaunting what I have, and he is a little boy left outside, impotent and bereft. He can see me but cannot get to me through the glass. He is humiliated and enraged and wants enviously to smash through and take back what has been torn away. Hence the compulsive and desperate, search-and-seizure quality of his addiction.

All parents effect changes, for better and worse, in their babies. To this extent they are loved, desired or dreaded. Where parents abuse or neglect, or are felt to do so, it may be this aspect of the relationship that is acted out in the repetition of early traumatic experiences in later dangerous behaviour.

Addiction to sexual love may be an attempt to put men or women into the position of the parent who excites us from depression, unworthiness and despair, in memory of a parent who was felt to tease and withdraw. Addiction to gambling, as Bollas points out, may reflect a conviction on the part of the gambler that the mother will not deliver the goods. Luck, be a lady tonight! Daniel's project is similar and is both memory and repair. In his addiction to food he stays close to the mother he lost, totally, at the age of two, and intermittently at the times of her depression. He cannot trust me to keep him in mind when I am not with him, and needs to prompt me to prove I will have something for him when he next comes. He seeks in the present a missing relational experience – that of consistent, continuing and reliable background care and attention – that will allow him to come to his own desires in his own time, confident that the need that arises will be met. This hope, he does not always dare to sustain.

When it comes to addiction to drugs, it is probably true to say that worried parents are fed, by media coverage at least, a kind of nineteenth-century diet. Certain magical properties are said to inhere in a number of pharmacological products that can alter personality and mood and render helpless all those who imbibe them.

> This mechanistic view of addiction is false but is sustained by press and media coverage, which regularly describes drug use in these terms. However, research evidence shows that the notion of the 'helpless addict' is functional, and that it serves clear purposes for people who are confronted by drug problems in some form. In other words, it is a useful type of explanation rather than a literal truth . . . Drug use derives from dynamic and purposeful, if unwise, choices made by individuals faced with particular alternatives. Consequently, understanding drug use requires a primary focus on the motives and intentions of people, rather than on the pharmacological properties of substances (Davies and Coggans, 1991).

Many drug habits, of course, are cultivated in the West by persons who regard themselves as normal and worthy citizens: tea, coffee, alcohol, tobacco. However, alcohol and tobacco are judged with extreme condemnation in other parts of the world.

> No simple pharmacological or physiological fact can provide the basis for a classification which distinguishes the drugs regarded in the West as illegal from those such as alcohol and tobacco that we accept and enjoy, or at least tolerate without legal sanctions. Consequently, any classification that distinguishes illicit drugs from approved or accepted 'recreational' drugs must be in terms of the ways in which we think about drugs, and our emotional reactions when the word 'drug' is used. For example . . . there is no simple pharmacological dimension equivalent to 'dangerousness' which separates the legal drugs such as tobacco and alcohol from the

> 'serious' drugs like cocaine and heroin. To all intents and purposes, alcohol and tobacco are quite definitely mind-altering substances and therefore 'drugs', yet psychologically they are not; we simply do not think of them as drugs in the same way as, for example, heroin or cocaine ... As a consequence, while we are quite happy to distinguish between the non-problem use of alcohol and its abuse, we do not apply the same criterion to illicit drugs. To use heroin or cocaine is to abuse it and the notion of normal or 'social' drug use cannot even be contemplated (Davies and Coggans, 1991).

The notion of benign addiction shows that drug addicts who inflict serious injury on themselves are as closely linked to normal behaviour as to anything psychopathic. The operative mechanisms are autoplastic. When life seems meaningless or hopeless, the addictive part of ourselves may seek through the use of certain substances to alter our perception of the situation rather than change the situation itself. Since our emotional life depends heavily on what we perceive, the use of chemicals to change perceptions can change how we feel. We believe the coffee, beer or heroin has provided us with emotional relief when in fact it has merely lessened the impact of a problem we took to be insoluble. It may still be hopeless, but it is no longer serious. This indulgence becomes rewarding, and is used increasingly when and before similar situations arise. When we were little and cried in the streets and shops, strangers would give us sweets (at home, we were told we were tired and were put to bed). Today when we are upset, someone makes us a cup of tea.

But why are we so horribly fascinated by stories of compulsive excess, so addicted to addiction? The subject seems to allow a symbolic dramatization of all of our relationships of love and hate. The drug that we read about or imbibe acquires its dangerousness by the projection of our sadism, our wish to cause pain and damage. It is endowed with the loving or hating characteristics originally associated with one or both parents and, as to those parents who were felt to be dangerous, through their actual menacing and abusive behaviour or by the projection of our own aggression, our attitude is ambivalent.

Drugs, like abusing parents, are hateful but needed. We are frightened of their power to hurt but require them for our self-esteem. The taking of the drug, then, represents control of the dangerous substance by incorporation, as in those primitive beliefs that an evil spirit or object, however damaging, can best be restrained by taking it inside the body; as in those other ideas that true love consists in swallowing that which one loves: 'I love you so much I could eat you'.

All of us are ambivalent about the people that we love. Some of us have internal representations of parents who really were violent or neglectful. Either or both of these experiences can be the source of the belief that we have bad things inside us. The drug that we crave anaesthetizes this inner badness or, since it is felt to be more powerful, defeats it. At the same time, the euphoria or relief from anxiety and guilt produced by the drug is a demonstration that it is a better and more reliable source of pleasure (and therefore love) than were the real parents.

When Daniel was taken into care at the age of two, his foster parents were unable to manage the method he had evolved to express and discharge his distress. They would stand helplessly by as he would storm to a furious climax, banging his head against his cot, pulling on his hair, digging his fingers into his skin or biting his hands, until he collapsed in spent exhaustion. The parent who let him down was never reliably available to receive and survive his screams of frustration and rage, and it was therefore as though Daniel acted out on his own body the violent attack he was unable to deliver to his mother. A fearful sense of responsibility for her depressive moods must have felt like mental torture. Her sudden disappearance was a pain too much to bear. The best solution was to torture himself and convert the overwhelming mental pain into a physical one that could be sexualized. In this way he managed to convert humiliation into exciting triumph, and his self-absorbed, masturbatory, masochistic state proved to exercise a hold that was stronger than the pull toward the uncertainties of relationships with other people – the frustrations and losses, the promises and disappointments. It continued into his day-long obsession with food, eating one meal while dreaming about the next.

But Daniel's love of eating is killing the body his mother made. He has already several medical conditions that are the direct consequence of his excess weight, and his doctor has warned him of serious dangers to his health if he continues to abuse himself in this way. Unfortunately, as any smoker will tell you, these warnings make the next cigarette taste even better.

Violence

In many dialects, and especially in the English spoken in the United States, the ordinary word for 'angry' is 'mad'. This revealing identity relies presumably on a notional equation of highly excited with frenzied or maniacal states of mind. The phrase 'losing one's head' refers literally to the practice of being beheaded, but has now acquired the figurative meaning of losing one's self-possession or presence of mind, and it is used to describe the highly charged feeling states of being in love or enraged. We seem to believe that strong emotions offer no knowledge of reality (perhaps we are right – reality is, after all, only a rumour). Mental health, we think, is best known or given in the absence, or at least the aftermath, of passionate commitment. Sanity is keeping one's head down.

If this is unfair, especially in the implied slur on such elevated and constructive moods as Buddhist compassion or Stoic concepts of apatheia, and the more ordinary experiences for all of us of balanced appraisal, it does nevertheless point to certain uncomfortable similarities between what we may take to be composure, that is cool at its points of collection, and self-control, frozen stiff in repressed fear.

Even-temperedness and good behaviour are sometimes sustained by the evacuation and projection of the more disturbing aspects of ourselves. In this way we create and need the criminal classes. An alternative and equally fair and effective method of dealing with crime may be to punish those who keep the law.

We are born into an intensity of need, bombarded from within by desire and pain and from without by stimuli we cannot control. Our absolute dependence on our carers makes us vulnerable to invasion or neglect by more powerful adults. Parents may be everything to the baby, but the baby is not everything to the parents. Carers have interests and problems of their own.

Absolute vulnerability in early relationships means the child can easily be exploited. Parents who abuse often have excessive expectations and demands of their children, finding it hard to allow themselves to be treated with what feels to be an apparent disregard for their own needs and wishes as people. Depressed parents, and those struggling to feel good about themselves, may take the infant's need to cry and be upset as an accusation, or as confirmation of their inadequacy and impotence, and they may forcefully suppress the expression of such feelings in their children. For the child, there is no distinction between the perception of an emotion and its expression. When expression is blocked or forbidden, nothing is noticed and nothing is felt.

Keith

Keith, age thirteen, was referred to me by the manager of a children's home where Keith had lived for two years. Repeated attempts at fostering had failed, and the social workers were worried that Keith's unpredictable outbursts of violence, combined with his moods of almost autistic withdrawal, would condemn him to a lifetime of institutional care.

Keith had been born by Caesarean section six weeks before term and had weighed four pounds at birth. His parents had been unhappy from the beginning of the pregnancy, and had both wanted a termination, but had somehow not pursued it. There were immediate bonding problems. Keith spent the first three weeks of his life in hospital because of low birth weight. On discharge he went to live with his mother, father, and eleven-month-old brother. One year later, another baby was born to the family.

When Keith was two years old, his mother asked for help with him. Bite marks and burn scars were found on his skin. He was placed on the at-risk register and then taken into care. Keith was fostered for five months, but his 'aggression to younger children' was quoted as the cause of several breakdowns of placement. After that there followed a succession of children's homes.

It was a depressing referral letter, but for me an increasingly familiar story. I found myself, as usual in such cases, skipping quickly through the information to defend myself against its impact. One paragraph in the history, however, forced its way to my attention.

When Keith was ten, he was apparently in the habit of stopping after school at a local children's playground. One summer afternoon he was playing in the sandpit when two parents arrived carrying a baby and walking their two-year-old boy. They told their son to stay in the sandpit while they went to buy ice creams.

Keith watched the parents carry their baby to the back of a queue at an ice-cream van. He then took the little boy's hand and led him across the park to a wooded area some distance away. One hour later, after a desperate search, the little boy was found, trembling and sobbing in the wood. His face was scratched, his clothes torn and muddy, and his mouth was full of leaves. Keith was back playing in the sand.

Keith and I met in the child guidance clinic where I worked. Keith managed to get from the waiting room to my office without once looking anywhere near me. He slouched in a chair, constantly moving position. I asked him what kind of a place he thought he had come to. He said it was a place to help. I asked what help he felt he needed. There was a long delay during which he stared at various objects in the room. Finally he spoke. 'Do you know Peter?' I said that I was not sure that I did. 'He asked me why there are no girls in Belvedere Close' (the children's home where Keith lives). Another long pause. 'How did you answer?' I said, not knowing where this was leading. 'I told him it is because it is only for boys.'

I was in danger of drifting off into space – there seemed so much of it around. Keith still had not looked at me. I asked him to tell me something about himself. Silence. I realized, belatedly, that my question had been a rather desperate attempt to find something solid I could hold on to, but this realization was not sufficient to stop me from following up with an even more fatuous question. 'Where do you live?' I asked him. I couldn't believe I had said it, but Keith looked unsurprised. 'Exeter, Taunton, London.' 'All those places?' 'Different children's homes. I lived with my mum since I was two.' It was clear that he meant that he had lived with his mother *until* he was two, but the strength of the irritation I felt, and my wish to correct or even humiliate him, alerted me to the kind of abusive relationships Keith had experienced in the past and seemed, therefore, to expect in the present.

He looked around the room as if for opportunity. To steal? Escape? 'Why can't you play computer games here?' he asked. Perhaps it was the accusatory belligerence of his tone that pressed my buttons. Perhaps I was still disconcerted by my irrational irritation triggered moments before. In any event, I heard myself making a speech in my mind with a passion I did not know I had on the subject. Because the universe of computer games is one-dimensional, I ranted at him sub-vocally. Because it is kill or be killed. Because it is the expression of an on/off mentality – right or left; jump or don't jump. Because the sounds and movements of these games are stereotypic, their rhythms mesmeric. Because, in front of these screens, you children become robotic and do not think. Because the world of these cartridges is autistic. Because it is self-enclosed. Because it leaves me out.

I tried to calm myself down. Keith had stood up and was examining a family of cloth dolls. I felt a strong personal need to account to myself for this internal outburst. I was all over the place and needed to recover.

In the fairy stories and tales of mythology that these computer games have replaced, I told myself, there was often a similar theme of a greater force being overcome by a lesser one. However, the smaller force would use strategy, cunning or guile. Its skills would be multifaceted. Most important of all, there were relationships, complex and troublesome, in which the characters were engaged. In this area of value there is between computer games and traditional narratives neither contact nor contest. The case for the defence having restored my psychic equilibrium, I returned my attention to Keith.

He had taken two of the dolls and was staging a computer game of his own in front of me. I smiled to myself at his loyalty to his desires, but my warm humour vanished as quickly as it had arrived. It was not the violence of the simulated fight that bothered me. That was just an amalgam of every cartoon battle I had ever seen on television. The problem was my sustained and violent exclusion.

At this first meeting, and then during every subsequent session over a period of many weeks, Keith demonstrated with the dolls his own version of the martial arts. Alongside there ran a commentary, or it could have been the voices of the contestants, which consisted of screaming prespeech sounds of unmodulated emotion which seemed like the chanted verbal equivalent of head-banging or the rocking of a caged primate.

Perhaps to Keith it was meant to be the foreign languages of karate and tae kwando. It was certainly a foreign language to me, incomprehensible and impenetrable, that served to underline and augment a barrier between us. Worse still, whenever I tried to speak to him, to ask a question or seek clarification, he would simply shout louder and force me to give up in defeat.

On one occasion I was delayed as we were about to enter my room together. Through the half-closed door I heard Keith begin his fighting game on his own. I collapsed into hopeless despair. What was the point of my going in? What difference did I make? I felt like the depressed or otherwise preoccupied parent who is forced to exploit his child's ability to amuse himself, to rid himself, without help, of his frustration and rage.

As I listened more closely, however, I noticed that the repeated sounds and phrases were now in English. I thought I heard 'Where is nanny? Where is nanny?' as though in some way Keith had allowed himself to register somebody's absence, opening up the possibility of symbolic communication between us.

It was at that time still rare for Keith to make contact with me directly. If, as in our first meeting, I failed to answer a question he put to me, he seemed hardly to notice. He had low expectations in terms of a response from others. His speech, such as it was, appeared always in monotone. I have no idea what mine was like. After an initial period of fury at being silenced and excluded, I felt mostly numb. My mind was empty as in the most superficial of attachments. I would treat him mentally, sometimes, as a kind of specimen, thinking, for example, that he would be the 'type' to refer to a therapeutic community.

Once, he sat before me and began pulling on a thread from his jumper. It elicited no symbolic association in me. I could think of no meaning for this and could not even motivate myself to try. I saw his action as potentially significant, but felt no inclination to pursue it. Like many of Keith's gestures or mannerisms it seemed senseless because in his early life no one had ever tried to make sense of what he did.

In these first months of our weekly meetings I had to work hard to hold on to my thinking processes. I sometimes was able to wonder to myself about these violent scenes enacted in front of me. Were they an externalization of his memory, or unconscious fantasy of the relationship between his parents, and if so, where did this leave him as the product of this relationship? If my feelings were any guide, he must have felt himself to be useless and helpless, a degraded and impotent bystander. Or were these battles a kind of protection of me, as though the fate of these dolls would have been mine had he not played the situation out?

Mostly, however, I had no questions. I felt only a kind of hopeless resignation. I wanted to get on with my own work, even though it held little attraction for me, while he played by himself. In no way was this Winnicott's child developing the capacity to be alone in the presence of an attentive, non-intrusive (m)other. Our separateness was not the solitude of health but the malady of loneliness, the loneliness that is felt most acutely in the presence of someone else's absence, in the forced proximity to a parent who keeps his distance to himself.

What sustained me was the belief that Keith needed to make me despair. He needed to make me feel as bad about myself as he did about himself. Only in this way could he believe that I understood him, that we were as one. In other words, his project was not simply to relieve himself of bad feelings in a way that despoiled me. Of course he felt he needed to rid himself of something frightened and frightening within him in order that the rest of him could live. But he was also trying to join and unite in the only way he knew. And there certainly was a change in our meetings when after some time Keith must have felt able to believe that his message had been received – that I knew what it was like to be him. I found myself, for example, spontaneously thinking about him between sessions in a way I had needed to force myself to do previously.

I had never tried to speak to Keith about the incident in the park that had happened three years before. There had been no reason to. Extensive work had been done by Keith and professional workers at the time and, even though his violence was still causing great concern to those who cared for him now, it was nevertheless clear that he had made some progress. More importantly, I try in general to resist the temptation to allow horrific or extraordinary events and symptoms to dominate my picture of another person, as though these awful things might somehow capture and define their essence. But, as part of the change in Keith that evoked reflective moods in me, I began to think how it might have been.

Perhaps Keith had tried to contact and rejoin the trusting, affectionate and vulnerable part of himself, awoken by the sight of a little boy left on his own, that he felt had been stolen from him. Perhaps it was important to make two parents worried about losing their child in a desperate, retrospective attempt to arouse concern in his own parents, who were felt to have failed to notice and respond to his distress and pain when he was little and needy. Such failure of empathy, combined with his parents' failure to recognize and receive Keith's hopeful and loving moves towards them, would have been experienced by Keith as a hostile rejection or violent attack, even without their real acts of violence perpetrated on him.

As the little boy is taken away, and fails to react happily and gratefully, his cries of protest and anguish are felt to be piercing reminders of how persecuted Keith feels by his own neediness which has never been received and made bearable by others. He feels driven to silence, and fills the boy's mouth with leaves to stifle the screams of the terrified abandoned child that threatened to put him in touch with that part of himself. Perhaps Keith's action was the disguised expression of a wish held long ago for someone to kidnap a sibling who Keith felt had stolen his mother's love. Perhaps it was the dramatization of the terrible judgement that the family is better off without him.

Infants have an innate reaction to turn their head away when stimulation from the outside is felt to be too intense. In this way they try to control or modify the output. There will, of course, be great individual variety in the degrees to which babies are sensitive to frustration and discomfort from internal and external sources and are able to tolerate such distress. In severe cases of neglect or abuse, however, babies and young children will numb themselves to protect their sensitivity from overload; they will harden up and become unreachable as the only way to defend themselves. When such numbing is prolonged and chronic, the growing person may later need to resort to extreme means to feel alive in the attempt to recapture sensation and feeling in parts of the body and self that have become anaesthetized. He may need to be violent in order to try to gain a response of recognition or validation, to force, finally, another person to do what he wants. His own sense of safety and power may depend on the projection into somebody else of his submissive suffering.

But violence is not only a phenomenon and consequence of individual history. It is also social and therefore more general. As part of his devastating criticism of industrial societies, Ivan Illich drew attention repeatedly to the dangers of a passive, consumer public, rendered stupid by disabling professionals. Health, for us, is really just another kind of patient role as we submit to the medicalization of all diagnoses. Health management, designed on the engineering model, conspires to produce as if it were a commodity something called 'better health'. Progress in civilization has become synomonous with the reduction of the sum total of suffering, with a resultant paralysis of healthy responses to discomfort, impairment and death. Politics is an activity aimed not at maximizing happiness but at minimizing pain. Pain is merely a passive event inflicted on helpless victims:

> With rising levels of induced insensitivity to pain, the capacity to experience the simple joys of life has equally declined. Increasingly stronger stimuli are needed to provide people in an anaesthetic society with any sense of being alive. Drugs, violence and horror turn into increasingly powerful stimuli that can still elicit an experience of self. Widespread anaesthesia increases the demand for excitation by noise, speed, violence – no matter how destructive (Illich, 1977).

Similarly, in relating individual lives of violence to failures in child care, we must be careful not to imply that even in the best of circumstances there is ever total parity of need and desire. In the parent-infant dyad, and other relationships between friends or lovers, no two people's desires or needs are likely to remain at the same level of intensity for prolonged periods of time. Ecstasy may be experienced at those points of exact confluence, in coming together, but there is a lot of other stuff to deal with as well.

> Kafka writes somewhere that the difficulties of the world are mathematical. Given the spreading out of possibilities along a plane, it is infinitely more probable that our paths will diverge rather than converge, that you will be out when I phone and I will be out when you ring my bell. Indeed, as Kafka points out, I was on my way over to your house at the time. If several conditions are necessary for success, and each is only moderately probable, the likelihood of their combination is wildly improbable. At every relay the message is distorted and we did not even speak the same dialect to begin with but just enough of the same language to believe that we both knew what we were talking about. A sudden stress or lapse makes me vulnerable to other lapses and so the rate of mishap is expotential. (Goodman, 1973)

I get out to change the tyre on my car and am run over by a truck. Disequilibrium is there from the beginning. This need not be anything to worry about as, from the parents' point of view, failure to anticipate and respond exactly to all gestures and desires is part of the repertoire. Trying to get it right, as much as you can, and seeking and accepting support is better than good enough. The difficulties and frustrations of relationships can promote in all parties an awareness of differentiation that can be tolerated.

Only in the most idealized accounts does mutuality in relationships imply exact mirroring reflection of mood and gesture. Reciprocity and mutuality between parent and child are made more difficult anyway because the parties are not equal. But reciprocity could only be said to have broken down between parent and child when the child loses over time the quality of relationship he or she needs to sustain growth. Parents may be depressed, deprived, or otherwise preoccupied and therefore unavailable. A better metaphor for good relationships may be that of a play of frictions. This need not lead to murder unless there is a felt tantalization that exploits a power imbalance.

Why violence?

From the child's point of view, and the child in the adult, there may be rage when the other person does not meet the need or share the desire. But rage, language notwithstanding, is not madness. Anger does not inevitably lead to violence. When held by the arms and minds of those who care for us we can allow our self-equilibrating mechanisms of shouting and screaming in fury to reconnect us to our other senses. With sufficient good experience of this we can learn to hold ourselves through anger.

Winnicott wrote of violent behaviour as a search in the present for an environmental stability that could withstand the strain of impulsive behaviour. In violence a person may be seeking a special kind of environmental provision that has been lost – an attitude from another of attentive containment, which, because it can be relied upon, allows freedom to move, act and become excited.

But all of us, in addition, are likely to feel an urge to violence when our environment does not reflect back to us the version of ourselves we seek to confirm. It is for this reason that it is difficult to demarcate an area that is specifically 'adolescent violence', that would relate to some notional 'age-appropriate' acting out. Such attempts are probably part of the project that universalizes the psychological adjustments to puberty as though they are the inevitable promptings of a biology that is flexing its muscles.

Nobody really can believe that it is *puberty* that causes young people to relive their past experience rather than recall it at this time, or that a new impulsivity overwhelms the thinking, speaking part of the personality and changes overnight the single and predictable child of latency into several mood-swinging strangers. (If it is true, so much the worse for latency!) Such theories are the remnants of a hysterical, unhistorical, presystemic approach that articulates the secret wishes of adults as they go to work every day.

Violence against homosexuals, racial minorities, or other groups, for example, is better explained by social and psychological theories of projection and scapegoating than by 'nature', whatever that is. In a society that dis-esteems the open expression of tender feeling, dependency and care, especially among men, sadism and cruelty may seem preferable to feeling 'queer'.

If we cannot tolerate disappointment and depression, then violent action may feel essential in order that no internal conflict is felt. Violence will therefore be the consequence of mental and emotional pressures, that we are unable to contain or express in any other way and will serve to release and externalize our pain.

When we lack self-esteem we may also act violently, although this may not always be a wholly intrapsychic or personal matter. When the stories we tell ourselves or hear are only of failure, and we see no hope for change, we may strike out in frenzied acts of reprisal. Not caring about what happens to others may be an act of identification with the judgement that nobody cares about us.

The young have the right to expect to be taken seriously and welcomed, and to feel they can 'come as they are' – as blacks, whites, Irish or Jews; as disabled; as boys and girls, young men and women. Their present deprivation is not so much the absence of rites of passage from childhood into the world of adult work, contribution and commitments; it is rather the original sharp divisions of these worlds in the first place, and the consequent fragmentation of the community.

There is no irreconcilable conflict between freedom and dependency, even if most of us struggle to move easily, to and fro, between these equally valuable aspects of being in relation to others. But we have somehow managed to sign up for a model of opposites in thinking about growing up that imprisons all of us in the rigid categories of adult and child, and the metaphors of emancipation and rebellion. 'The young always have the same problem – how to rebel and conform at the same time. They have now solved this by defying their parents and copying each other' (Crisp, 1968).

There is such a tension, and not only for the young, between belonging and individuation, but defiance and imitation could hardly be said to constitute much of a solution. Presumably, the 'not so young', to finish the story, no longer defy but only copy.

5
Groups

Naomi

Naomi is a child of the dream. But this dream, she says, was dreamed by somebody else. 'I was born on a kibbutz during the War of Independence. Soon after my birth, my mother was sent by our kibbutz to support another, where she stayed for several months before being able to return for a visit. My older sister believed my mother was dead. I knew nothing of my mother's absence until told much later. We lived, even as babies, all together. Our parents would visit and take us home for the afternoon, but we would sleep in the children's house. At first we were a group of six babies, but by the time we were school age, our number had risen to twenty-four. I grew up with the idea that it was very important to be a part of a group. It was the epitome of fulfilment. To this day I cry when I see or hear tales of people uniting together in common struggle, in protest and liberation; or in the construction of projects and movements that are important to them. I love it and I believe in it, but I find it so hard to do myself.

'The adults who founded the kibbutz believed that children are a part of the community and should be raised by the community. There was the added benefit that parents could also be freed for work and could have a greater private life of leisure and recreation. It was a lot of fun. As teenagers, we slept three to a room, but I remember never wanting to share a bedroom with my best friend. I was frightened our friendship could not survive this extra and extended intimacy. I treated the boys as brothers and was never attracted to any of them in a sexual way. We children discussed with our teachers until what age we should take showers together, and we decided we would do this up to eleven years old. I never had a boyfriend from the kibbutz.'

In the famous study of life on an Israeli kibbutz, Spiro (1958) observed young children who lived together in a children's house, similar to the one in which Naomi was raised. He noticed that the boys and girls engaged in a considerable amount of sexual play. They kissed and hugged each other, and examined one another's genitals, in a game known as 'clinic'. But by the age of twelve, these children had become reserved and nervous in the same company. By the age of fifteen, the relationships were like those between brothers and sisters. These young people were not related by family, and were therefore not subject to any of the usual prohibitions against incest. Spiro found, however, no evidence of any marriage, or even sexual intercourse, between members of the same children's house.

In a follow-up investigation published thirteen years later, the sociologist Shepher (1971) examined the records of all known kibbutzim marriages. Of the 2,769 that were recorded, he found that only thirteen marriages were between people from the same peer group.

Naomi's sexual excitement was located in her fascination for the volunteers, especially those from North America. Their status on the kibbutz was unclear, and they were not always favourably regarded, but Naomi perceived them to be open and free, uninhibited and direct. She loved also the foreign language they spoke. For much of her adolescence she was in love with many of those who passed through the kibbutz on working holidays.

She was friendly also with those within the kibbutz but on its margins. One new member criticized the kibbutz in a public forum and was consequently ostracized by his fellows. Naomi, however, sought him out and would wait every day to eat with him in the dining-room. She kept, in addition, the company of those who had mental health problems, or those who found it difficult to mix with others.

She was herself mainstream, but befriended those at the edges. She lived at the centre, but knew herself always to be radical. 'Many adults looked after us when we were infants but one woman, the mother of a good friend of mine, was a special influence. When I think of her, I begin to feel very sad.' She falls silent and looks away, her eyes moist with tears. There is a moment's pause. Then she gathers herself together, apologizes for the interruption, and continues, perhaps by way of explanation. 'Whenever I talk about my childhood I feel sad and I don't understand why. I really don't understand it.' She repeats several times that she does not understand but there is no appeal for help. No one can ever explain. It is up to her to know.

'I have been in groups all my life, but I have always felt completely on my own. I am a very social person with good social skills. I like people and I am kind, but I feel such a distance. It is as though I am two people.' I ask if the two people that she feels herself to be could be her parents. She is interested in my question and I feel intelligent. I radiate self-esteem. 'You are right. My mother was warm and lively and engaged well with others, whereas my father was more stern. He always seemed to be looking on, as if from some distance away. And yet I always felt I was his favourite, the one he regarded as special.'

She remembers a relative from the same town in Poland as her mother. This man would stay with her parents when she was little and would bring a present for the children. Whatever he brought Naomi, would always evoke from her the same reaction. 'I acted as though this was the best present anyone could have ever bought me, as though I had been waiting for this one gift all my life. I knew it would make him happy. My mother was amazed. I was only six, but I felt even then that I could never trust anybody with my real feelings. I was the only one who could deal with my issues and concerns because I was ashamed to think that others might know about them.'

I tell Naomi that I think she is warning me to be thoughtful about the presents we try to give each other. I am the man from Poland. From her isolation and mistrust, she may be driven to make me feel happy about what I give her. In this way she will continue to be left on her own, but secure in the secrecy of her own thoughts and feelings. She laughs generously in acknowledgement. For a moment I am overwhelmed by envy. I feel in the presence of somebody greatly superior to me, somebody who can smile fondly at her own exposure when she has been found out, a thing I can never do. My experience of her seems to contradict the account she gives of herself until I realize that my own feelings of inferiority and shame are probably stimulated by a similar state of mind in Naomi, that she presently represses and evacuates.

I am astonished at the strength of the impulse within me to tell Naomi all my thoughts. I feel the desire to talk at length about myself to this very good listener. As I reflect on this, a related association comes to her. 'When I went for my admission interview to study psychology at university I managed somehow to get the interviewer to talk about his own dreams. I myself said almost nothing. Afterwards he praised me for such an interesting discussion, and said what a rich cultural background I was from! When people praise me it is for nothing that is really in me. They praise only something they see in me. I do nothing but reflect a fantasy of theirs.'

Naomi feels herself to be the blank screen on to which the uninvited project their dreams. Her true self must remain a well kept secret, lest the expression of her own feelings make more difficult the intrusion of the feelings of others. There are aspects to her, she has decided, that nobody should ever know about. She feels she has never had a single person she could talk to. She is afraid. 'What people see of me on the outside is not what I am like inside. If they knew what I really think and feel I would be vulnerable. I would be humiliated. Only a part of me is ever involved in any activity.'

I think to myself that I am somebody Naomi could talk to, but I notice that she speaks always *of* other people and not *to* me. I am intensely aware of her and of myself in some kind of relationship to her, but the mood is of an intimacy that is at once evoked and evaded, as with those members of the group, or neighbours on the street, who seem always to be deliberately looking the other way. It is 'nothing personal', and yet only that. I cannot tell whether Naomi's description of herself as unknowable contains a desperate plea to be contacted, or is a statement of triumphant victory. My thoughtful silence has clearly unsettled her. She speaks in her agitation as if to seek reassurance but leaves no space for it. Her questions are rhetorical. They do not need to be answered. Perhaps they are not really asked.

'I don't know what I am talking about, I really don't. I am ashamed to say that I think other people should always validate what I am saying, you understand? Doesn't everyone else feel the same? It's funny. I don't go to certain clothes stores because everyone else does, and yet I want everyone to be the same as me. It is as though I need to make myself different in a symbolic way. Then I feel outside and do not mind. I never feel safe enough to be *really* friendly with anyone. For me, the important thing is that the other person likes and enjoys an experience with my being there, rather than that I like it. I am always the listener because listeners do not have to speak.'

'How does the child discover himself within his mother's care without losing himself to her?' ask Greenberg and Mitchell in their paraphrase of Winnicott's questions about infancy and early childhood. 'How can the child differentiate himself yet retain maternal resources? How can one communicate without being depleted, be seen without being appropriated, be touched without being exploited? How can one preserve a personal core without becoming isolated?'

Naomi remembers the fears and nightmares of her childhood on the kibbutz. There was an old man who was ill. Naomi was frightened that if she touched him or went near him she would herself become ill but she could never tell anyone. She looks up and away, into the distance. I remember her description of her father. Her smile is sad. I think of a little girl who looks up to her father and is troubled by what she wants and what it may lead to. She is fearful of a bad thing that she thinks she has already done. What other secrets are we frightened to tell?

She remembers dreaming that her parents were sitting next to her. Sometimes she was unable to fall asleep until she could convince herself that they were beside her. She pauses and falls into a reverie. Somehow, and for a little while, I feel included and alongside, the parent who allows his child to feel safe and let go. Suddenly and

> violently, Naomi wakes us from the dream. 'I feel stupid. I feel my story disappoints you. That is why I am always the listener.' It is an extraordinary misunderstanding, a ruinous misreading of the situation. Before I can recover, however, Naomi is already moving on.
>
> 'I can always support others but cannot ever take personal initiative. I join groups but never belong. I seem to have to find someone within the group that I can believe in. Then I will go along with the group and even use my own thinking. But the cause that we fight for remains always in the rightful possession of the others and is never mine. It is loyalty to the other group members that keeps me involved in the group. Without this I would withdraw. I always stay detached and am not wholehearted, whereas the others seem totally committed. I do not feel brave enough to take initiative. I never trust that what I have is good enough. I need a strong leader next to me to be able to do anything.'

We are on familiar ground. In our gangs of nation, church, political party or street corner, we identify with our leader and participate thereby in her power. In addition, and in needed contradiction, we gain personal favours and prerogatives while at the same time submerging our aching and isolated, shivering and separate selves. In bending our will to our all-powerful and all-knowing leader's wishes, we can repair the narcissistic injuries of our infancy and live once more the dreams of glory. As before there is maximal devotion. Somebody is absolutely worshipped; somebody is absolutely indulged.

It is sympathetic magic. The leader is both parent and baby. The follower is the same. By our participation in the ritual of following leaders we can enjoy by imitation the idealized version of our parents as people who put aside their own wishes and desires in order to facilitate and gratify ours (or better yet, as people who did not even have different wishes of their own that needed to be put aside) and at the same time punish them for their failures and the falling away of their total preoccupation, by doing it better ourselves.

But the illusion of idealized parents needs to pass and our grief must be expressed. If not, commitment may come to represent a terrifying entrapment of pathological symbiosis. We may feel in great danger of losing ourselves, smothered and unable to breathe. There must always be available a route of escape. We join in but do not join.

How does it come to be this way? It is clear that in regard to Naomi, with her capacity to interest and be interested, it is not a matter of neglect or poor attention. Perhaps, in reverse, her parents failed to disillusion her and left her feeling she was too central and important to them, always their special and favoured one.

Naomi's parents were pioneers. They had escaped from centuries of persecution to build a different world. They wanted to be, and raise, different kinds of people. For them the kibbutz was part of the movement of protest against the values of the nuclear family with its project of individualism, its promotion of class separation and isolation. They believed they could throw back the past and create something new.

But theirs was some past to throw back. Naomi's parents were themselves raised in families, and the inherited mythology would have been very strong. Furthermore, the kibbutz existed within a predominant set of cultural attitudes in Israel and the diaspora, which continued to proclaim the importance of Jewish family life. It is impossible to believe, in this beautiful and inspirational first-generation experiment of commitment to the social and community care of the young, that the transmission of family-type values and loyalties could have been absent from determining influence.

Naomi, herself now a mother, imagines the conflict for her parents' generation who had to leave their infants to the care and company of others for extended periods, and the consequent pressure on all parties to ensure that visits of the children to their 'homes', be acknowledged as times of quality and intensity. Adults may be free to work and relax, but they may miss their children. They may also be guilty about leaving them.

> 'It's funny. When I talk about my childhood and adolescence, I expect to talk predominantly about my peer group. Others would expect this too. For most people it must seem such an exceptional experience. But I find myself always talking about my parents. Of course the group was important, but there were many other influences as well, especially my relationship to my mother and father. I grew up in a group because that was where I was put. But I am sure my parents must have felt themselves to be torn between loyalty to the kibbutz ideal and their love and need for their children.'
>
> She was in the children's group, but a part of her had to believe she was not really there. Her parents' division within themselves is lived out by Naomi. She is in the group for somebody else, but must not for the same people surrender herself fully to it. She feels she must now help group leaders, in the way she once helped her dreaming parents. For myself, I confess to a belief that the kibbutz is one of the great achievements of our time, a design of heroic proportions. At every meeting I sustain therefore the private hope that Naomi will in illustration, perhaps of some present difficulty, speak of her formative years in that place of *my* dreams, as well as those of her parents. When she does, however, it is often with proffered mood of

hesitation or reluctance. 'I feel so ignorant about the history and beliefs of those who founded the kibbutz. I should know more because this is my life and the life, also of my parents. This is my childhood and my adolescence. It is impossible that I do not know more and yet I do not.'

Probably we repeat together the original situation. I want to hear the stories of good experience, of how perfect was her childhood in that place of grand pledge to community living. The likely consequence is that my interest re-stimulates for Naomi, the pressure to reassure her parents, that their dream has not been her deprivation. The gaps in her knowledge and description, her faltering performance of celebration, are both her loyalty to their own doubt and ambivalence, and her unconscious anger and resentment towards them.

She makes her own contribution, of course. Her subjectivity and demandingness are projected into me in order to keep the screen blank. She senses my interest and adds then her own, which serves in turn to fuel and magnify mine all the more. As she encourages me to feel good about my vitality, she enjoys her creation of another's entitlement to bask contentedly and proudly. She has found a safe house for her lively, desiring self that is felt to be too troublesome or destructive within her.

In her present social life, Naomi slips quietly and unobtrusively alongside her identified leaders. These people represent her once idealized parents and the once-idealized aspects of herself. When she supports the leader she can repair the image of an incompetent parent who has fallen from grace and she can put right, vicariously, her own shortcomings and failures. If she contributes to repair or success, she cannot be the cause of the damage. Unconsciously she continues to believe that she has hurt her mother and siblings, in rivalrous competition and victory, through being the light of her father's life. If she keeps to the wings she can feel the agonies of her punishment.

But symptomatic behaviour is the secret gratification of a wish. It is disguised fulfilment. The fact of her self-imposed punishment proves she really feels herself to have been successful in her forbidden desire. Similarly Naomi makes clear her ambivalence to the leader and the group when they fail to acknowledge her as the most important one. She makes promises that she does not deliver, forgets agreements and is always late. She feels awful but does not change. I ask Naomi to tell me a story of her life that will make sense to her of all this. She says she really doesn't know. There is a silence in which the clear task for me is to stop myself telling her my own life story under the guise of giving her an example of how to go about

> it! When she begins to talk there is again a sense of compliance, of going along with what I want. After all, what do you tell a psychotherapist except tales of your own childhood and your earliest memories? But as the story unfolds, I have again my own ideas about her rich cultural background.
>
> 'Our house was at the very end of the kibbutz. The children's section was separate from the adults. I would have to have run a long way to my parents. Behind our house was the fence and behind that were the fields. At night I could hear the jackals crying like babies. We children lived out collective fantasies. We believed there was a witch who came every night to disturb us. We resolved to pretend to fall asleep in order to catch her. For a long time we never managed to stay awake but one night we succeeded and we actually caught her. It was the poor watchwoman!'

Of course I notice, in her memory, the crying babies and the absent mothers, the separation from the parents and the wish to run to them. When the good mother is longed for but absent, the bad mother/witch is present and must be confronted. But these are details of the story. The irresistible impression is of the fun, creativity and camaraderie in this group of children who lived and slept in their own house. Here is the counter to the gloomy *Lord of the Flies* scenario about what happens when children are together. The important distinction, of course, is the concerned and watchful presence of adults who are there to respond and protect, but who can let the children be.

> Children are capable of positively curative effects on one another when their relationships are allowed to evolve naturally. There are limits and exceptions and I am not speaking here of children thrashing about in a vacuum of neglect, but working out relationships against the background they are entitled to expect of adult protection and concern. By 'natural' I mean such situations as we ordinarily observe when children are at play – without adults. The first rules of behaviour we teach our children, far from being mere maxims, are immediately and profoundly functional. The child sees he must share or the activity will cease; he must honour his agreements or the game will end; he must show consideration or he cannot have friends. As soon as children are placed in schools or other situations deliberately organized for their benefit, we suddenly act as if they had no capacity at all for the practical sociability we have aleady seen. We place all decisions in the hands of adults and prescribe what they shall play and for how long and how they shall relate (Dennison, 1970).

David

I watch David from my window as he leaves the classroom in the special school and makes his way towards the psychotherapy room. It is the longest distance between two points. He crosses the playground and ambles towards a group of boys gathered in a huddle near the gate. Technically they are within the school grounds, but even I, who have neither responsibility nor authority in regard to their whereabouts and behaviour, am unable to watch them without a rising anxiety that they are about to run out, or begin some other delinquent act.

As David approaches, there is from the group a welcoming fire of expletives. I hear '. . . your mother!' called our several times by different boys. Their faces are fixed in expressions that lie somewhere between a smile and a scowl. The insults are their handshakes – the kind that reach for you firmly, and hurt.

David punches one of the boys on the shoulder, then lunges towards another in an attempt to grab something from him. For a few moments all boys push and jostle together until two of their number separate out, the one in the headlock of the other. They fall to the ground, kick out as they stand, and then return to the group which had not even turned to watch.

A circle forms. No one is still. In turns and in ones or twos they step or stumble into the middle and then leave again, as if in a square dance. One sways to a music that only he hears and another pulls at the crotch of his jeans, in a gesture of careless sexuality. Their labelled trainers and jackets are untied and unbuttoned, as though it is a matter of indifference whether this expensive uniform is worn or discarded. The open defiance of their parents' routines of careful dressing takes the form of a casual disregard.

The poignancy of the whole experience does not escape me as I watch, in my middle age, from behind glass and from some distance away. I could despair of their cruelty sometimes, and their scorn for those who do not, for their purposes, belong, but there is no denying the warmth and vitality of these young men who are so loyal to their drives of sexuality and aggression. They explore each other by touch and prod, by nudge and punch, ignoring or overcoming resistances and inhibitions, with a curiosity excited by their narcissism. All the more disappointing, then, is the ferocity of their compulsive heterosexuality and slavish hatred of homosexuals.

The group disbands with the arrival of a teacher, and David resumes his journey my way. At each step something of the confident swagger falls away, until a self-conscious and embarrassed teenager takes his usual position in the room, shoots me a furtive look, and looks down at the floor. We both wait for me to speak.

What makes him attend every week, this boy who breaks every rule and is on the point of exclusion, even from this compassionate and tolerant school? Why does he do this one thing his mother asks of him when he takes such little notice of her other requests and demands? He has brought shame on his religious family with his repeated brushes with the police that culminated in a recent caution. I smile to myself as I remember his answer to my question at our first meeting, when I asked if he knew why he stole: 'I just like to have a little money in my pocket,' he said. It was obvious and it was true. Who is going to say that it is not something worth wanting? But it is probably the only completed sentence he has spoken in a year of weekly meetings. And it is certainly the longest one.

The disparity between David's and my speech habits is always with us, but never more so than at the beginning of each session. Our talk is of our own kind. It does not join us together, but serves to bind and define us as members of our respective gangs – his, the adolescent group on the street corner; mine, the class of psychological youth managers. Our language asserts our group identity at the time that it commits us to it. It is both emblem and pledge. It is our badge and our oath of loyalty.

David's utterances crack like machine-gun fire in short, staccato bursts. When he speaks I cannot approach because I am pinned to the wall behind me. But at my words, in turn, he winces in pain and retreats. We enact together a ritual of gabbling speaker and inattentive listener. Once, in response to a request from David that I change his appointment day to the beginning of the school week, I began a session by apologizing that I could not manage Mondays. 'Me neither', he replied. I was puzzled as this was the particular day I thought he had insisted on. He seemed to be unaware of my confusion until I referred to it. 'I can't manage mummies neither', he said.

David uses only active voice and it is rare that he will amplify or embellish with adjectives or adverbs. I vary my speech moods and sometimes use expressions like 'It could be thought that . . .', or 'One sometimes finds oneself . . .'. He deals in facts, whereas, and especially when I am with him, I feel I am nothing more than the sum of my opinions. But his comments are peppered with phrases like, 'You see', or 'You know what I mean?', as if he continually needs me to tell him that I understand what he is saying and he is doing all right. I fight an urge within me to judge his speech less clear or worse than mine, when in fact he makes himself known to me just as well as I do to him. Both of us are doing fine.

Sometimes, through my middle-class spectacles, I see David's uncertain pronouncements as signifying his doubt as to whether he has any place or stake in the world that he can declare. I after all take for granted that what I say reflects or changes reality simply by being said. But there is another possibility. David knows what belongs to him, and does not feel that speaking is the way to lay claim to it. What David has is the evidence of his senses. I have sat in several meetings where his worried parents have harangued him about the sexual and other adventures he has been involved in with his friends when truanting from school. By threat and argument, plea and bribery, they have tried to persuade him that he does not really want to do what he is doing, that he does not really like it. They seek to wear him down by their persistence, to bore him into submission. David has told me that this happens all the time at home. He has, I know, very different musical tastes from my own and fondly disparages the singer-songwriters in my theatre of heroism, as the same breed of ageing hippy that he thinks I am. Nevertheless, all of these artists have probably composed any number of verses on David's plight that would gain grudging acknowledgement from him that they understand what it is like. Each time David tries to leave the house he is crossly examined. When he returns, he is charged.

David's parents and teachers are entrusted by the adult community with the responsibility of securing from him an admission that there are better things for him to do than 'fool around' with girls. He of course knows that nothing could be better – certainly nothing else that he has seen on offer in the world he is expected to live in.

The saddest thing is that the adults know this too, hence their inability to stop going on about it. But it leaves David in a difficult position. If he surrenders, denies his own experience, and complies through love and fear with the official view that the best way for him to spend his time is to sit still all day in classrooms, studying subjects that do not interest him, in preparation for meaningless jobs that do not exist anyway, then he sustains an unarticulated conviction that the adults around him are fools or liars. He will also believe that his body gives him misleading and dangerous information.

The alternative may not be much better. If he continues in his ways and 'will not be told', then the unconscious fantasy which drives us all – that what we like is bad for us and is in any case forbidden – receives, in his case, the external confirmation of the law and its enforcement agencies. He will be punished. Perhaps he will be sent away. Not satisfied with this, we may further discount his universe by telling him that what he thinks he likes is a disguised search for the more important experiences of love and care that the rest of us took for granted in our childhood; that he sexualizes (and therefore trivializes) his relationships to deny unmet dependency needs; that he has been led astray by the wrong kind of company he has been keeping, or the wrong kind of videos he has been watching.

I am not saying that such considerations as these are never relevant nor true. Of course they are. The problem is in their application to particular cases. I am suspicious in myself of a particular kind of puritanism that kicks in when I look at other people's lives that are different from my own, haunted and obsessed as I am by the idea that someone, somewhere, might be having a better time than I am. It is probable that this clouds my judgement somewhat.

David's parents and I would agree with Jean Cocteau's dictum that vice is vertical – if David is having sex then he is probably up to all other sorts of tricks as well. But I, at least, am bothered (and amused) also by the observation of Quentin Crisp, that 'vice is its own reward'.

> Is it an eccentric opinion that an important part of the kids' restiveness in school from the onset of puberty has to do with puberty? The teachers talk about it among themselves, all right. (In his school, Bertrand Russell thought it was better if they had the sex, so they could give their undivided attention to mathematics, which was the main thing). But since this objective factor does not exist in our schools, the school itself begins to be irrelevant. The question here is not whether the sexuality should be discouraged or encouraged. That is an important issue, but far more important is that it is hard to grow up when existing facts are treated as though they do not exist. For then there is no dialogue, it is impossible to be taken seriously, to be understood, to make a bridge between oneself and society (Goodman, 1960).

This is undoubtedly a strong possibility but the issue is much wider. The apparent 'restlessness' of children of all ages – their wandering around and reluctance to sit still at desks – is taken by school inspectors and government ministers as a certain indication of some problem within the child or failure of the teacher, rather than the reassuring demonstration that they are still alive. Everybody seems to believe that children can and should be 'managed' out of their wish to explore and move freely, as if learning can only take place when all are stiffly quiet and facing in the same direction.

The meaning of groups

The difficulty with those stories of young people written within the psychoanalytic tradition is that they can appear to suggest that the formation of groups is a universal intrapsychic tendency of individuals in adolescence, as though some kind of instinctual reflex or reaction to the maturation of the sex-specific hormones. Apart from the fact that most adults you speak to have no memory of going around in groups at that time in any different respect from the way they do now or did as younger children, i.e., for specific events or functions, it seems as likely that those who do spend time in groups or gangs are seeking some sense of belonging, validation and recognition from each other to compensate for a real sense of being excluded from the possibilities and priviledges of the grown-up world around them. At the same time they are forced to suffer the indignity of an increasingly lengthening developmental apprenticeship from the time of the maturation of their bodies until they are legally entitled to a free decision as to their use in work or recreation.

In other words, if it is important for us to learn from Blos (1962) that the peer group in adolescence may be an important place for the displacement and resolution of dependency needs that can no longer be met or satisfied within the family – even if it is an odd idea to think of dependency needs as something one would ever 'resolve' – and that the group's leader and principles are often invested with the power and status once granted to the parents. It is equally important to acknowledge that exclusive peer association may be forced on many young people by the dominant adult 'compact majority' (Ibsen, 1982) that does not want them, because it still needs them to carry certain feelings and carry out certain actions on their behalf. After all, we do not claim that it is somehow in the nature of ethnic minorities that they are disposed to live in ghettos.

It is a sad fact that our schools are set up to fail young people, despite the best efforts of the individual teachers and other adults who staff them. We compel by law participation in this obstacle race for many young people whose desires, talents or aptitudes are better suited for the kind of work or experience that schools cannot provide. We then subject them to feelings of humiliation through the clear implication that whatever they themselves enjoy, or are good at, is of lesser value than success (measured in terms of triumph over others) in the subjects of the National Curriculum as taught in the classroom.

If the young were allowed into the pubs, clubs and places of work that are presently the exclusive preserve of adults, we would none of us allow such places, and the practices that pertain within them, to continue as they are. Similarly, if adults attended the schools as voluntary pupils, to learn and study alongside the children who wanted to be there, oppressive practices of group management and bullying could be addressed and resolved in very different ways. There will perhaps be different issues and problems, but they are likely to be ones the community will be able to solve for itself as it applies its collective intelligence and wisdom.

Of course we need to recognize that one feature of group life can be the socialization of guilt, where a gang may perpetrate together forbidden acts that its members as individuals would not commit. There is nothing specific to adolescence about this and contrary examples of people combining to achieve constructive goals that alone they may neither contemplate nor manage are as common. But the idea still prevails that groups of young people are up to no good.

Meltzer (1967) wrote that the typical adolescent gang has five members. I presume he meant that in this way such individuals exhibit together some kind of unconscious shared admission of the centrality of manual masturbation in their lives at this time. If ever you find youself standing at a party or conference with four young psychoanalysts, leave at once!

6
Idealism

'When it comes to adolescence, we feel hesitant,' wrote Anna Freud in her classic paper of 1958. It is a promising start. We, of course, are grown-ups, adjusted and adapted, realistic about ourselves and others, and clear about what is possible. But hesitation is conflict. She continues:

> I take it that it is normal for an adolescent to behave for a considerable length of time in an inconsistent and unpredictable manner; to fight his impulses and to accept them; to ward them off successfully and to be overrun by them; to love his parents and to hate them; to revolt against them and to be dependent on them; to be deeply ashamed to acknowledge his mother before others and, unexpectedly, to desire heart-to-heart talks with her; to thrive on imitation of and identification with others while searching unceasingly for his own identity; to be more idealistic, artistic, generous, and unselfish than he will ever be again, but also the opposite: self-centred, egoistic, calculating. Such fluctuations between extreme opposites would be deemed highly abnormal at any other time of life. At this time they may signify no more than that an adult structure of personality takes a long time to emerge.

It is a brilliant paper, with important observations about the struggles of growing up. But a question remains – implicit perhaps in the last sentence of that quotation – that is the subject and substance of many jokes, and no less true for that. Which of us who is still alive is not adolescent? 'At sixteen I was stupid, confused, insecure and indecisive,' said Jules Feiffer. 'At twenty-five I was wise, self-confident, prepossessing and assertive. At forty-five I am stupid, confused, insecure and indecisive. Who would have supposed that maturity is only a short break in adolescence?'

Something at the centre of the issue is revealed in one of Anna Freud's most unhesitating pronouncements in her paper: '. . . adolescence constitutes by definition an interruption of peaceful growth.' Winston Churchill might have added: 'some peace, some growth'.

Conflict and idealism

Conflict is integral to growth, especially where that conflict is allowed to rage and is not suppressed for the sake of a quiet family life, when enforced peace is sustained by shared but unacknowledged fears of total destruction. Conflict begins on day one, and the capacity to tolerate it will be internalized from parents and others who demonstrate the ability and willingness to look at their own pain, acknowledge and express their own anger, and allow others to do the same. It is unlikely that the physiological event of puberty will, of necessity and for purely intrapsychic reasons, involve conflict that is excessive to any greater extent than any other struggle. To the extent that it does, the causes are probably to be found in the teasing ambivalence of a culture, in family and society, that excites passionate sexual and aggressive feeling but disesteems its overt expression as action.

The critical issue is the fate of the child's intense love for the parents at puberty. In our social arrangements, it is certainly the case that the nuclear family will provide intense and prolonged contact throughout infancy with one or two adult figures who attract the full eruption of desire. The parents are unable to fulfil the wishes so aroused, and, as young people mature earlier but are required to spend an increasingly lengthy period of time in the dependent relationships of their families, there is a problem to negotiate.

The optimal outcome is for this gonadally driven love to be directed towards other people outside the family. Where this route is blocked because of anxieties and inhibitions, the love remains within the self: 'Clinically this means that ideas of grandeur will appear, fantasies of unlimited power over other human beings, or of major achievement and championship in one or more fields. Or, the suffering and persecuted ego of the adolescent may assume Christ-like proportions with corresponding fantasies of saving the world.' (Freud, A. 1958).

John

John is a first-year university student with a story to tell. He sees himself in a room with beautiful paintings. As he describes them, he pauses to remember that there is a technical name for this kind of picture. He says something in French and asks me to confirm that this is correct. I cannot imagine another situation in which such a question would not have triggered in me the laughter of unease. I strain at all times to appreciate and understand the visual arts. Children in psychotherapy with me paint in the first session and then never again. Every muscle ache, every lumbar pain, which is the consequence of our species move to upright posture, overtakes me inside an art gallery.

But it does not matter to John. The interruption is barely noticed. His eyes are bright and wide. He can see the room as he describes it, and I can too. We are transported, seamlessly, into another place. 'I am beautiful', he continues. This is true. I look or stare at him sometimes in awe and reverance, probably with the same expression that he has now as he visualizes the scene. 'People come into the room. They move towards me. But slowly their faces change from total appreciation to the beginnings of concern. They seem to find a flaw in my appearance. It is my sadness. At this moment my keeper arrives to distract and pull them away. They are told that I am fine and can be left alone. There are other beautiful exhibits that they really must see.'

John is the oldest of three brothers. The family is from Northern Ireland. His mother died when he was a child, and his father brought the young family to England via New Zealand and Australia. John has an all-consuming interest in politics. He wakes every morning in a mood of anger and incomprehension about the state of the world. He cannot understand why everybody is not devastated and furious, how they can continue their daily lives when everything is so awful, so clearly wrong. The newspapers and other media fuel this rage with every item they report. But it is not just the content that disturbs him. In form, the news broadcasts themselves are a collective thought disorder. One tragedy after another, with no connection between them, is delivered in clean and presentable form by clean and presentable people who take no responsibility, show no emotion and allow no space for reaction.

'It is,' he says, 'as though every few minutes your doorbell rings. Each time you open the door a different pleasant-looking stranger tells you how many people have just lost their jobs; how much poverty, violence, abuse and racism exists in your neighbourhood; then they wish you a nice day and leave.' But there is something that John has not said and it relates, in a way, to his story. He tells himself that he could not bear it if the world were to be as horrible as it appears. Something is wrong, but there is a paradise somewhere. He cannot see it but is compelled and obliged to create it. I ask him to tell me about this paradise. I am not sure whether he has heard me.

'I was seven when my mother died. I was on my way home from school and saw a group of people outside my house. My father ran towards me and picked me up. I was crying even before he told me. I cried and cried until I caught sight of my little brother, who was holding my uncle's hand. I never cried again.' He remembers the days and weeks of sympathy and kindness, at school and in the street. It was a small community and everyone knew. But even at that age he became aware that there was something in his experience that was strange and did not fit. He began to be unsure about the reality of his feelings, unclear about whether he was just making everything up.

John supposes now that he had always thought himself to be his father's special child. They look very similar, both of striking appearance. He is sure there was a golden age in the early years of his life when his father, who was himself raised by a single mother, worshipped and adored his first-born son. It is the love, care, excitement and contentment of this period that he feels he must ensure for all mankind in his political ideals.

I point out to John his use of the language of obligation and compulsion when he talks of the world he would like to see. John is irritated and seems to sulk. I feel I have spoiled something in the mood or atmosphere of his story with a clumsy, irrelevant and selfish interruption of my own. He says he cannot stand it when people do what I just did. Why did I have to stick my oar in? He was in the middle of something that was important to him, and now it was ruined.

His manner is cold, his expression angry and hurt. He looks as if he is considering walking out. I cannot decide if I want to slit my wrists or punch him in the face. It feels impossible to believe we can recover from this, and yet I do not think I have done anything so terribly wrong. It is the time for patience and courage. Fortunately, John has made no move to leave and this frees me sufficiently of anxiety to sift through my thoughts and feelings and try to decide which of them may relate to John.

It seems a fair hypothesis that John believes, or has been led to believe, that he is somehow responsible for the spoiling, ruination and loss of paradise. Hence the sense of obligation to repair or recreate. But John shows me what it is like to feel ambivalent about apology. We both desperately want back something that has been lost, but we are unclear what we have done to occasion this loss in the first place. The power of the accusation disposes us to believe we must be guilty. Probably it tunes in to every unconscious fantasy of being at fault and to blame. However, to restore in these circumstances the beautiful moments that have gone is to let somebody else off the hook. This may be something we are not prepared to do.

In the minutes that have passed, it is apparent that John has been working too. His demeanour has changed and he looks approachable. Perhaps I have to be first to break the silence, but I no longer mind. I ask him to say more about his father. There is a slight delay, long enough to make the point. I like his pride. 'With my father, I never knew what was true and what was just a story. After my mother died, we travelled a lot as my father had done when he was a boy. I did not want to go to school again, and for a year my father kept me from it. He said that I would have a lifetime of school, routine, work and obligation, and that children should be free. I was excited and inspired by the power and delivery of his view. Inside this aura, I felt special, privileged and different. Later, when I started school for the second time, I suspect that my reluctance to attend, from the first day to the last, was that I never stopped being the new boy. I never became a part of the group. I felt detached from the ordinary life of my peers. I was an outsider, as was my father. We were always looking in.'

But looking in is always looking up or down. As John speaks, I feel dull and boring. My clothes seem scruffy and unkempt. I suppress with difficulty a wish to slouch lower in my chair. I despair of my 'normality'. He is continuing to speak, but each sentence has to fight its way past the word 'ordinary' that hangs as a curtain of judgement between us. I strain to listen and realize he is talking about the same thing.

He is remembering a playground in a primary school. All around him children are running and laughing. He is at the edge and alone, his back against the outside wall of a classroom. His eyes are turned in longing towards the school gates. He cannot understand how his father could have left him here. Surely he will come now to take him away, to take him back home? He wills his father's appearance at the gate and at moments seems to see him until the adult that approaches becomes an old man with a dog, or a lady carrying home her shopping.

It is every story of exile and banishment. John tells of the cold shadow that lies outside the radiance and radius of his father's love. He has been sent away, then robbed and stripped of what he thought was his, of what he thought distinguished him, by this school that suppresses or eliminates difference. He chokes back a rising envy at the carefree children around him who seem not to mind. They play with abandon while he can only suffer it. But now, and in this way, his father answers the call and is with him, as he summons his disdain. The group is a herd. These other children can be as they are because they do not know any better.

John smiles sadly at the memory and lapses into a silence that is comfortable and productive. Within it, it is easy to think and take stock. We have assembled together a picture of a father who was ambivalent about his special attachments, and was troubled by the love he felt for his children. Perhaps he envied John for having a father, even though the father happened to be himself, and sabotaged his parenting to get back at the father he never had.

We imagine this man as a little boy, inventing stories in the spaces of the sort of dad he would like to have, based probably on the best aspects of his relationship with his mother. We see him next when he is a parent himself, seeking to reproduce this idealized father-son relationship with his own children. But something always goes wrong when we try to realize our dreams by force, or to sustain and preserve a vision of consummate beauty by denial and suppression of the flaws or imperfections that threaten to spoil it. If John's father himself had in his imagination a father who was perfect, he would have had also, in the shadowy recesses, a figure who was hated for his absence, an absence he would have construed as motivated by a selfish and uncaring lack of interest. These two inner representations would need to be kept apart for fear that the hatred borne out of lonely experiences of disappointment and loss would destroy the sustaining and nourishing ideal of the faultless father within.

John knows that the problematic aspect of his political idealism is his identification with his own father's conviction that painful emotions are unbearable. In his tireless commitment to the causes he believes in, he finds continually that he takes on more and more of the work. 'I just don't seem to notice that others are suffering and falling by the way. Or, when I do notice, I feel they are being self-indulgent or accusing me in some way.'

Suffering and sadness spoil the beautiful painting. But John is in psychotherapy because he recognizes that the picture is incomplete. It cannot be right that he is privately so in touch with his own grief and distress, yet not noticing or intolerant of the feelings of others. Or that his own moments of unhappiness are only disguised attacks on his father. He knows, from the many good aspects of his father's care, and the compassionate response of his community at the time of his mother's death, that suffering is meaningful and can be survived with renewed growth and strength. The central sacrificial moment of Christianity, to which Anna Freud alludes, does not grip the imagination of both believers and doubters as a story of masochism, but as a statement of the affirmation of faith and conviction, and a striving for the ideal.

John knows also that the inspirational vision of his father that fired him with a standard and memory of what is possible because it is already real, does not need to be discounted simply because it struggled to incorporate the dirt and mess of artistic creation; its dreams and disappointments; its achievements and losses. It just needs more work. 'The day is short, and the work is great, and the labourers are sluggish, and the reward is much, and the Master is urgent. It is not your duty to complete the work, but neither are you free to desist from it' (Rabbi Tarfon [Avot 2:15]).

Linear models of development do not match our experience and need cautious application. Idealism, for example, is commonly associated in psychoanalytic writing with late adolescence. In this way it can be disparaged and treated as something to be grown out of. If we deal in this way with idealism, we need no longer be bothered with ideals.

By the time of their late teens or early twenties, some young people might have adjusted to the changed body that has brought them into line with their parents and other adults in terms of strength, size, and capacity for procreation, penetration and orgasm. Adaptation to a changed body requires the integration of a new body-image into the image of the self. Where this is achieved, we might expect a decrease in the preoccupation with the body-self. A browse through the magazine shelves of any newsagent, or half an hour in front of the television will show us that few adults actually let up on this obsession. Nevertheless, when adolescent thoughts are dominated by the changing body, it may take one or many of several forms, unnoticeable or obsessive from the viewpoint of the equally preoccupied observing adults: food fads; extreme personal modesty and disgust with the parents' clothes and tastes; anxieties about appearance (as, for example, where acne is felt to be external evidence of dirty or disgusting thoughts or fantasies); asceticism or chronic boredom as the attempt to keep, or consequence of keeping, forbidden and threatening temptations at bay; hypochondriacal fears about the genitals or, by displacement, other parts of the body; or a strutting and proud exhibitionism to replace the previous high valuation of the parents' bodies and capacities.

In addition, in those families where rebellion against and withdrawal from parents and their internalized values surfaces only at puberty, interest and concern may be directed outwards into social and cultural values and ideas (in most families, it has probably been there all the time, as anybody who actually listens to children will know). Older adolescents may become interested in morality and religion; for example, Starbuck quoted in Hadfield's book (1962) on childhood and adolescence, states that the average age of religious conversion is sixteen.

All such interest in politics, morality and religion is part of the process of establishing personal standards and values. For all of us, cynicism and hopelessness often alternate with renewed waves of idealism, in the wake of the repeated discovery of the discrepancy between how the world should be and how it actually is. One problem for adults with the idealism of the young is that the latter have the unfortunate habit of insisting on a searching examination of the moral probity and lifestyle of their parents. They like to compare the deeds and actual behaviour of the grown-ups with the beliefs that they claim to espouse. Parents and society, as a consequence, may be seen more objectively. Failings, hypocrisies, compromises and complacency can be more clearly apprehended.

We adults sometimes claim, in our defence or just defensively, that young people attack everything *because* it is old. We discount their apparent 'solutions' to social and world problems because they are too simple and clear. They do not do justice to the complexities of 'real life'. If their proposals were taken seriously, we might have to give something up, or change.

All of us, in our tentative and sometimes painful strivings to be the people we want to be, and to live the lives we want to live, seek cues from those around us. We try to establish or infer what kind of people we are from the way others regard us. But we seek also, both openly and secretly, suggestions and models that we can adopt and emulate. There is often in this area a kind of adult embarrassment about admitting to the conscious selection and imitation of the traits or activities of people we admire, as though it were something essentially juvenile. If it is indeed something that young people do, so much the better for them.

The rest of us may live instead in an age of cynical suspicion. This is fuelled by the newspapers who sell copy with the latest revelation of the hypocrisy or fall from grace of public figures, who are caught doing the very things that they have denounced as moral degeneracy. The saddest part of all this is that it serves to rationalize fears of commitment to our own improvement and to the improvement of the society within which we live. 'We cannot look, however imperfectly, upon a great man,' wrote Thomas Carlyle, 'without gaining something by him... I consider hero-worship to be the grand modifying element in the ancient systems of thought... No nobler feeling than this of admiration for one higher than himself dwells in the breast of man... Hero-worship endures forever while man endures.'

I agree, although we are not speaking here, of course, of the idolatrous adoption of only one person and everything about them. Such a tendency, in young and old, must certainly relate to a reluctance to relinquish idealized versions of the parents and ourselves. Idealization is a defensive response to ambivalence and is sustained by the creation of somebody or something that has to be, in contrast, totally bad:

> Idealization differs from admiration in that the idealizing person needs a perfect person to exist and ignores the existence of those attributes of the idealized person which do not fit the picture... it leads to dependence on and subservience to the idealized person and not to emulation and imitation... Idealization, especially of the parents, has a vital part in the setting up of the ideal agencies within the subject (Ideal ego, ego ideal) but is not synonymous with the formation of a person's ideals (Rycroft, 1972).

Some of the feelings, then, of loving and being loved, attach themselves to ideas or causes which can then become ideals. For young people like

John, who were held in some passionate relationship to one or both parents, the commitment to an ideal may help to fill the empty space that is the consequence of increasing distance from the mother or father. The ideal may be a kind of spiritual substitute that is neither uncontaminated by sexual elements, nor excites forbidden action.

To have an ideal, it is, of course, necessary to be able to think on an abstract level. Inhelder and Piaget (1958) maintain that the attainment of formal operations is a hallmark of cognitive development and occurs in the individual around the time of puberty. Thinking becomes less concrete and more abstract at this time, and the development of abstract ideation furthers individualized thought and the reassessment of values. Those older adolescents who remain in further education are certainly encouraged to think in concepts and to hold and measure them in their minds. They are expected to entertain several apparently conflicting ideas at once, without simply accepting or rejecting any or all of them out of hand. Matters of philosophy or politics may be the stimulus for a great deal of debate at this time and humane causes are sometimes pursued that involve considerable conviction and sacrifice.

But context is everything. Whether psychologists recognize their cognitive development or not, or believe even that they have the capacity or life experience to make complex moral judgements and decisions, prepubescent children, as well as older adolescents, are often fighting at the centre of idealistic campaigns of great human significance. Many young people, who were barely adolescent, were in the forefront of anti-apartheid action in South Africa. Children take part in the political struggles in Northern Ireland and have fought and died in many parts of the world in the last decade:

> But this involvement in the adult world is not a recent event. The Children's Crusade of the Middle Ages mobilized thousands of children from eight years old and upwards to march hundreds of miles across Europe with the idea of recapturing the Holy Land for Christianity. The leaders were not adult exploiters but twelve-year-old boys like Stephen of Cloyes. In the same era, boys of that age recruited and led armies and were responsible for major state decisions. (Ennew, 1986).

All through my primary school, my best friend was Wallace Mitchell. His family were Scottish, his father was the manager of a local farm which had somehow continued to survive on the edge of the London suburb where I lived. The farm and its houses seemed even then to be curiously anachronistic; incongruous and out of place.

Wallace and I were inseparable, not only through a shared passion for football. I remember being interested, always, in his opinions, and I sought and trusted his judgements, more probably than those of our teachers or the other adults of our acquaintance. I was troubled by his scepticism about religion at a time when I was a firm believer; troubled, but comforted also, by his fierce sense of justice. Once, near the railway track, we fought, and I wrestled Wallace angrily to the ground. Two men who were repairing some fencing along the line ran over and remonstrated with me. I was ashamed and frightened. Wallace told the men that he had provoked me, and that the fight had therefore been started by him. It was true. In the face of critical onslaught, I had either not remembered, or had thought it not relevant to say.

When we were nine, our classes were streamed according to somebody's notion of academic ability. Wallace told me some weeks before this was due to happen that he could predict which children would go into the top class by the quality of clothes they wore. I remember on that occasion laughing out loud at what I took to be this absurd proposition, so seriously delivered.

Probably there had been occasions before in my young life when I had thought the world was mad. I know I had sometimes entertained grave doubts and misgivings as to whether the grown-ups knew what they were doing, whether they were really worthy of the positions of authority and power that they seemed so confidently to assume for themselves. But if I had felt such things previously, it had never been with the degree of force and conviction that was about to hit me on the first day of the next school year. I looked around the class for Wallace. He was not there. I was in the upper class, he was in the lower.

It was awkward, but we managed it somehow. I needed to adjust to the idea that this wise and sensitive friend was not so 'clever' as I was. In retrospect, his apparent resigned acquiescence was more worrying, although at the time I was rather in awe of it. We would, anyway, meet at break-time, after school and at week-ends, to play football and cricket, to hang about together.

The day that notification of our Eleven-Plus examination results arrived by post, with its consequent implications for our secondary schooling, another friend and I walked over to the farm. We discussed on the way our thoughts about whether Wallace had passed or failed. When we arrived, none of us was able to raise the subject. Finally, I asked Wallace if the mail had been delivered. 'I am going to the secondary modern,' he said at once, knowing exactly what I was after, 'but I will be following a grammar school course.'

I felt humiliated by my own success, which seemed so hollow now, and sick with the embarrassment and deceit of it all. A desultory attempt at optimistic conversation ensued and we headed for the park, probably in an effort to forget the whole separatist nightmare and replace it with the dream we could share – team-mates at Arsenal, stepping out together onto the Wembley pitch for the Cup Final.

It proved difficult to sustain the friendship when we began our secondary schools. I forgot Wallace's twelfth birthday party (for which his mother had prepared a special tea) because I was at the house of a new friend, a secure member of the social class I was aspiring to join. When I saw Wallace some days later, he said that he thought I had not come to his birthday because he had burst a plastic football of mine the week before.

We met less and less over the next few years, and I was always uneasy if I saw him on my way home, especially if I was in my school uniform. Once, aged fifteen, I saw him with his school friend as they waited at a bus stop and I stopped to talk. The friend recognized my blazer and said he knew my school because his uncle worked, in some capacity, on its sixty-acre estate. He was generous in his praise of my school's playing-fields and modern buildings, its many facilities and its atmosphere of rural peace. I tried to change the subject, but Wallace's friend was clearly trying to establish a link with me, and must have felt that this was the way to do it.

Finally, as I feared he would, Wallace interrupted. 'Do you think it is fair, Paul, that some children go to schools like that and others have to go to places like ours?' The friend would not let me answer and leapt in to defend me, succeeding only in making it much worse. 'I think brainy kids deserve better schools than us. They need good places to study and get on.' 'I don't agree,' said Wallace, as he looked behind him, toward the bus that was coming to take them away somewhere.

Wallace left school at sixteen and took a job in a local menswear retailer. I dropped in one Saturday morning to see him, and he told me, as he pretended to sell me some shirts in order to fool the watching manager, of the songs and poems he was writing. He had a friend who worked in a London hotel where famous singers stayed, and Wallace hoped his friend could show some of these performers his songs.

The divisions between us were by now so deep that it was impossible even to listen without feeling I was patronizing him. I knew this was the fault of neither of us, but felt nevertheless trapped and paralysed, unable to change or refer to it. My enthusiastic and encouraging expression felt false and frozen, stuck to my face, and I was worried he would stop talking and tell me to go. In the event he seemed not to notice, and continued excitedly to speak of his plans. Finally, he asked me what I was doing that evening.

I don't remember what I said, only that it did not seem like very much. I was certainly not intending to boast. But whatever it was, his recognition of the difference between us stopped him in his tracks. He looked as if I had slapped him. I asked him what was the matter. 'I don't know. I was shocked by what you said. It seemed you had been waiting for me to finish speaking of my silly dreams, so that you could tell me about the really important things you do all the time.'

It was the last time we ever spoke. Some weeks after my eighteenth birthday, I had left my school but needed to return there to collect an examination certificate. I sat in the tiny office of the school prefects and made conversation, 'old boy' and out of uniform, with a prefect I had not known very well when I had been at the school. He asked if I had heard what had happened there the previous day. I said I had not. 'Somebody drowned in the swimming pool.' I was shocked at a death in the school and assumed the person who had died was a pupil. I asked who it was. 'He wasn't from here. One of the other prefects knew him and said he was a bit of a yob.' The next day, a short item in the newspaper, announced that Wallace Mitchell, aged eighteen, had been found dead in the swimming pool of my old school. He had broken in with two friends late at night, and when these young men had looked for him to leave, they had found Wallace lying face down in the pool. 'A bit of a yob.'

It was thirty years ago that he died, and I think about him at least once every week. Sometimes a memory is stimulated by the struggle or plight of a young person with whom I am working; sometimes a mood of my own, of panic or regret, of vulnerability or incomprehension, triggers a chain of association that plunges inevitably toward a death in a pool, that scene of haunting unrest in many of my dramas of exclusion, privilege and difference. And I know that other stories begin or end there as well and jostle for position, influencing in subtlety and variety, the direction and intensity of the feelings evoked; those stories of love and loss, of hopes and dreams that were lived or dashed, of childhood and growing up.

Within the world that I inhabit today, friends and colleagues are greatly worried about a growing underclass of alienated and disenfranchized young people, who see no future for themselves, and who are teased and discarded by an economic system that promotes in glossy packaging commodities and personal constructs that become shabby, shoddy and obsolete by the time those who can afford them have left the shop.

'Why do I insist on the article that "all men are equal?" ' asks Paul Goodman (1969), the practical utopian, the idealist, the common-sense extremist. 'Perhaps because I am afraid of the Unchosen. My behaviour, a kind of incognito, looks like protective coloration.' Perhaps. But it would be character assassination of the grossest kind to reduce concern for our young people to a simple fear of their envious attack, as though we do not recognize morality and idealism as achievements, but instead only as points on a scale that extends from complacency to enlightened self-interest.

Destructive envy and jealousy, triumph and guilt, are emotions with which we struggle from early in our lives and will therefore form part of a complex friction of forces within us in our interactions with others. But gratitude, concern, empathy and reparation are also essential constituents of our experience. Those who see cruelty in children are speaking really of the absence, in some, of the use of face-preserving social conventions. Children who believe themselves to be participating in their parents' omnipotence, through wishes of their own or adult reluctance to disillusion them, may feel little need to protect their vulnerability in social situations and may therefore give no thought to handling others in a gentle way.

But we see much else in young children as well; their sense of decency, symmetry and fair play, learned in the home and generalized out into their relations with their peers. Where these qualities are allowed to flourish, in communities that include and respect individual difference, children are idealists long before puberty, with clear views about what is wrong and what should be different. The source of hope throughout life, wrote Joel Kovel (1981) the radical psychoanalyst, is the experience of reliable goodness in infancy which becomes a kind of loving inner companion who can be mobilized in difficult times. The child, young person or adult with ideals, seeks only to universalize the care she received in her early life.

7
The Mood

'Let us treat the men and women well, treat them as if they were real – perhaps they are.' Ralph Waldo Emerson (1906)

Erik Erikson (1973), in discussion with the Black American political activist Huey Newton drew, attention to our tendency to focus solely on the *child's* hostility in the central psychoanalytic concept of the Oedipus Complex. But what about Laius? Is it the same complex, in the adult's memory, that makes him so ready to believe the oracle when it predicts that the boy will one day kill his father? Why did the king believe in his son's potential threat rather than trust his own ability to bring up Oedipus and prove the oracle wrong? Some of us have been so preoccupied with the sons who want to kill their fathers that we have failed to recognize the fathers who want to sacrifice their sons. But not all of us.

Oh God said to Abraham, 'Kill me a son.'
Abe says, 'Man, you must be puttin' me on.'
God say, 'No.' Abe say, 'What?'
God say, 'You can do what you want Abe, but
The next time you see me comin' you better run.'
Well, Abe says, 'Where do you want this killin' done?'
God says, 'out on Highway 61.' (Bob Dylan)

The name of Abraham's son, Isaac, derives from the Hebrew word meaning 'laugh'. Abraham is 100 years old and Sarah, his wife, is barren. God tells Abraham he will give him a son by Sarah.

> Then Abraham fell on his face and laughed, and said to himself, 'Shall a child be born to a man who is a hundred years old? Shall Sarah, who is ninety years old, bear a child?' And Abraham said to God, 'Oh that Ishmael might live in thy sight!' God said, 'No, but Sarah your wife shall bear you a son, and you shall call his name Isaac. . . . And Sarah said, 'God has made laughter for me; every one who hears will laugh over me.' (Genesis, 17, 18, 21, 6; Revised Standard Version).

The biblical story continues to evoke the ambiguities and ambivalence at the heart of the relationships between parents and children, between young and old. We laugh not only in celebratory joy, but also in patronizing amusement and ridicule as the young strive to be old and the old 'pretend' to be young. We smile as the children talk like little grown-ups; but there is no fool like an old fool. This intergenerational trial of love of the Old Testament, whose central character is the figure revered by the three great monotheistic religions, is a lesson in filial trust and paternal conspiracy to murder. It is the sons, Isaac and Abraham, who follow in faithful devotion, and the fathers, Abraham and Jehovah, whose thoughts are of killing.

The name Oedipus means 'swollen foot', which in the story is the consequence of the little boy's rejection by his parents when he is tied to a stake, abandoned and left to die on a hillside. But in a reverse reading, as when we search for meaning in the interpretation of a dream, we could think of an appendage that swells up as the *cause* of a child's rejection.

The thought of children's sexuality, it has to be said, makes everybody want to take to the hills. In an abstract sense it is possible to grant such a thing, but only, of course, with other people's children. Largely, the imagined threat must be to the breakthrough of incestuous ideas. But it is harder, also, to sustain the combination of innocence, happiness and powerlessness in our notions of the young if we attribute to them sexual feelings and intentions; and innocent, happy and powerless is what we need our children to be:

> We live under the assumption that children are especially privileged and that our entire culture is 'child-centred', but the 'romantic mythology' encrusting childhood is very much like that used for racial and gender power-moves: 'children, people of colour, and women are all depicted as naturally carefree, fortunate to be unsuited to the burdens of autonomy and decision-making, and better off protected by those in control' (Kincaid, 1992).

The 'protection' and control of women was something highlighted by Levi Strauss (1969). He argued that women are always minors because they have no status other than as the daughters or sisters of men. To this extent they are social children, but with built-in exchange value, the consequence of their being swapped or passed around by their fathers or brothers in the ceremonies of marriage. Their dual position consists, then, of sex object and minor, the critical factor in their oppression being who is in control of their sexuality.

The women's liberation movement has successfully challenged patriarchal authority by enforcing the recognition of women as subjects of their own desire and agents of their own actions and decisions. Those adults, in contrast, who act out their ideas in regard to the sexuality of the young are no allies of youth. Incest maintains, in the most extreme form, the family's command over its children, whereas paedophilia is another version of oppression, in which children are viewed only as sex objects exchanged by men.

The rest of us may not like to think about the sexuality of our children at all until, of course, they reach adolescence, when we can think of almost nothing else. Perhaps like Laius we have the idea that it can bring nothing but trouble – best turn a blind eye and hope it goes away, or rely on a little unconscious communication to get the message over that it really is not very nice. Sexuality is too imperious, clamorous, urgent and insistent to allow to those in junior positions. Our belief that it is for these reasons disruptive of order and authority turns up in those organizations that forbid people 'in relationships' from working together, especially where there are issues of hierarchy or management. It is easy to understand why. With its overcoming of self-and-other resistance, its closure of distance and its naked elimination of difference, sex is the equalizing goal. When two people make love, other people are left out, and we know also what we ourselves become in our secret affairs – liars and cheats; ruthlessly focused, obsessive and irresponsible. Just like children, or so it appears:

> Infantile structures of the personality . . . are dominated by self interest and the impulse to avoid pain. The sexuality of those structures is propelled by jealousy, envy, greed and competition for the pleasures which the child believes the parents enjoy and which are denied to him. It tends to be accompanied by a sense of grievance based on lack of recognition of limited capacity. . . . Infantile sexuality is essentially concerned with getting pleasure and gratification in omnipotent ways, by bodily manipulation or phantasy. It is characterized by the child projecting himself into the phantasied secret relationship of the parents . . . in various ways, and with varying degrees of illwill and non-acceptance of the fact that he has to wait to be grown-up, and that being grown-up means carrying responsibilities, notably babies, as well as enjoying power and privilege (Harris, 1987).

The psychoanalysts have made it difficult for us to think of our children as innocent, which makes more difficult our demand that they be happy. But to be compelled to be happy is, even without this, quite a pressure, for them and for us. They are to be new productions of ourselves as children, of course, and they are most at risk from the imprisoning effects of such projections when we are dissatisfied, frustrated and disappointed. Since we do not like ourselves in these moods, we can hardly like anybody else:

> It is clear that the myth of childhood happiness flourishes so wildly not because it satisfies the needs of children but because it satisfies the needs of adults. In a culture of alienated people, the belief that everyone has at least one good period in life, free of care and drudgery dies hard. And obviously you can't expect it in your old age. So you must have already had it. This accounts for the fog of sentimentality surrounding any discussion of childhood or children. Everyone is living out some private dream on their behalf (Firestone, 1971).

Sentimentality, said Winnicott, is repressed hatred. If in a sentimental mood we give to our children with one hand, they can be sure we will slap them with the other. 'The profession of teaching had its first crude beginnings in the tortures, humiliations, instructions and, to us, immoral ceremonies of the initiations into manhood and womanhood' (Hollingworth, 1929). This history lesson may have little to teach many young people today.

The idea that our children are changelings who at puberty 'come out' as different personalities is probably a survival in folklore of the ceremonial rebirth which constituted the formal initiation of our ancestors into womanhood and manhood. In public ceremonies the child was 'made over' socially into an adult, and this social change has become equated or confused with notions of biological change:

> With the advent of puberty, the child was considered adult in privilege and responsibility. The years of growth and change which follow, and which civilized [sic] people call adolescence, were and are usually disregarded in the practices of savage [sic] tribes. The boy become a warrior before he was fully grown. Girls became wives and mothers at an age when we now regard them as little more than children (Hollingworth, 1929).

It appears that in ancient public ceremonies many of the most conspicuous tests of maturity – of fitness for adult life – were examinations of the young person's capacity to suffer. Physical and mental hardships were inflicted as ordeals, and the boy or girl who raised an outcry, refused the ordeal or yielded to fear or pain, failed the initiation. Three significant beliefs, with modern ring, can be assumed to have informed these practices: that suffering is a cardinal experience of adult life; that emotional maturity consists in an extreme form of fortitude; and that childhood, in opposition, is pleasure.

However, when we adults look back longingly towards this lost golden age of childhood with its excitement and happiness we either enjoy the search with lascivious anticipation, or we see paradise itself as a place of sensual pleasure. How else would we know about it? Why else would we yearn? Its appeal, and our attraction to it, are the same.

The problem that confronts us is what to do with the belief that if something is pleasurable, it cannot be innocent; and that if it is not innocent, it cannot be happy. Happiness and innocence seem to require, as in Eden, the separation of the pleasures of naked bodies, from sexual interest and knowledge. Unfortunately, that garden centre was closed down by Freud.

> John is home alone. He is fourteen, or thirty. His parents/partner/children have gone out. He turns on the television and turns it off again. He tries some music, on record and radio, and looks for somebody to telephone. He thinks about a cup of coffee. He is restless and uneasy in a familiar way. He wanders, with script of aimlessness, to the bathroom, and looks in the mirror. He undresses and masturbates.

This is sexuality, the motive for and quality of, our curiosity and awareness. This is the mood, a haunting erotics of change, absence and loss. We cannot really know *about* other people's sexuality, including that of children. We can wonder only about our own wish to know, or not to know, and the form taken by our research.

Rambling through the Elysian Fields of an imaginary lost childhood is the pastime of our age. The narrative is, of course, a delusion of our own childhood in which we 'remember' ourselves as the focus of devout parental worship. It is ourselves as Narcissus, central character in the myth of exact and loving mirroring. Our parents were never able to sustain such excited delight in us. Why should they? The myths deal, therefore, with the feelings that are denied and split off to create this idealization – the hatred implied in the cruel ignoring of Echo. Echo is castigated for her intrusion into a marriage of the gods – she interferes in the marriage between Hera and Zeus by supporting the adultery of Zeus. She is guilty, therefore, of the fulfilment of an envious Oedipal desire. Echo's punishment is to suffer the fate of the child who is excluded by the self-obsessed nostalgic dreaming of vain adults. Like the infant, she has no speech of her own (Latin 'in-fans', meaning 'non-speaker') because, like the child, she can speak only when spoken to. She cannot speak for herself. She is helpless and hopeless, therefore absolutely dependent in her longing for acknowledgement and recognition.

If we adults seek by way of selective memory and yearning to make our children into reflections of our dreams of primary value, we will need to deny their subjectivity and agency; to control their sexuality through subtle disparagement; to leave them out.

It is hard to wish those we love, our partners and our children, to be free and strong. There is the danger they may then be excited and exciting with other people besides ourselves, have opinions of their own, live their own lives rather than ours. If as the best compromise we can manage we can keep them innocent and dependent, we can be secure, if a little bored. Perhaps they might play in the playground, while we take a snooze, or daydream on the bench.

We endeavour, therefore, to 'protect' certain aspects of the energy and enthusiasm of our children but restrict others. It is an impossible project, of course, and our ambivalence continually defeats us and them. The colonization of childhood becomes ever deeper entrenched; independence day, an increasingly receding promise in the future. Children are allowed every freedom except the essential one of being allowed to grow up and decide how they want to spend the time and money of their own, that we do not believe they are ready yet to have. They never finish going to school. They are locked in an eternity of envious longing towards the world of the grown-ups.

Similarly, we set free much of the boisterous barbarity of children and then make our towns and busy streets too dangerous to explore. The children are forced to live in the cramped spaces of tower blocks or concrete estates, and play in the local playgrounds, that may meet the latest health and safety regulations, but offer little to the curious and lively child we have 'created'.

Melanie Klein's child, however, resists all attempts at idealization. S/he keeps us awake and on our toes, either pushing the swing or, at least on the other end of the see-saw. S/he is much more recognizable to babysitters and childminders, more in touch with primal sympathies, more complex and threatening. Her child is opinionated; actively benevolent and malevolent; compassionate, but full of hate. S/he is, therefore, better companion and opponent, more substatial participant and contestant; a person, already, who makes demands and resists control. If we can keep this real child better in mind, we are more likely to keep our projections to ourselves.

> Simon, aged fifteen, tells me he has two faces; one is real, one is a mask. In a literal sense it is palpably untrue. Simon, like everybody else, has as many 'real faces' as he has emotions. When he is angry, his real face is of rage; when he is happy, his real face smiles. Sometimes, when his self is hateful, I sing to myself in fretful reassurance, a line from the song by James and Atkin (1974): 'Take off your face, I want to see the mask.'

I know, of course, what Simon means and why he wants to have one real face. It feels essential to believe in and have recognized a core self, a central and pervading sense of unity. We are troubled and blush at charges of inconsistency, of acting out of character.

As a consequence, perhaps, there is a favour we are only too willing to grant in our social interfaces. We are delighted to take any opportunity to let other people know what *they* are *really* like. But it is not only the others who are deprived, thereby, of our attention. In failing to get to know them we refuse also a fence of self-knowledge; we are ourselves other people; or, as in this case, they are us. Adults would support Simon's view of the number of faces that he has, although they would disagree with him as to their composition. For most of us, apparently, youth does indeed have two faces, both of which present images of deviancy. Young people are depicted 'as either uncontrollable and violent, or as flamboyant and outrageous promoters of fashion and subcultural style', views supported by two surveys of the way in which adolescence is reported in newspapers.

> In spite of increasing contradictory evidence, the storm and stress image of adolescence appears to be a particularly powerful one. It is important to remember that it is within this social context that adolescents are developing their identities (Falchikov, 1989).

And not just adolescents, of course. The overlay of cultural suggestion is present for all of us in growing up from birth to death – boys and girls, men and women, young and old – with particularly vicious consequences for visible minorities, who get landed with the projections and punishments of societies that complacently exteriorize unacknowledged divisions in the soul.

Two of the disparate faces of psychology have a bearing on this. One stresses the consequences for identity, of the birth of the infant into a preformed human culture that is ready and waiting to pounce. According to this argument, the symbolic world of the child is necessarily built from the outside in. The child identifies with the attitude to herself of other people, primarily her parents, and in this way, in this order, and in this first foreign language, she gains awareness of her 'own' feelings. Her self does not come into being without other selves as authors, witnesses to the dramatization and performance of a script that is written by them.

Since she must first identify, her identity is a social creation. She will be her mother and father before she becomes herself. She will take up residence in her own body only after weeks of external survey, during which time she will be staying with her parents while they move in the furniture and fittings. Her identity is therefore, of necessity, alienated.

The other line of thought places greater emphasis on the primacy of corporeal experience in the growth of psychosomatic union. Despite depending, it is of course conceded, on the empathic recognition, response and reflection of its carers, certain initially fragmented or unconnected feeling states, felt internally through proprioception, perception and movement, will cohere for the child into a sense of self that feels real and is centred within, firmly rooted in the body. The parents are inside, but more in the sense of a pervading style that ministers to, decorates or adorns, something that is clearly felt to be the 'true' self. These two ways of thinking reflect the dualism of experience that people often report, and inform the best approaches to parenting style, educational and therapeutic practice.

It is clearly the case, as Winnicott and others have demonstrated, that a child's self-image will be greatly affected by the perceived demeanour of her carers. How she feels about herself will reflect the attitudes and anxieties of those closest to her. She may identify with a mother who forbids sexual exploration and pleasure, or a father who prohibits tears, or screams of rage.

Where a child's outgoing actions are interrupted by the disapproving restraint of powerful others, she has to put herself in somebody else's shoes before her own have been provisionally selected and tried for size. She takes on the role of the other person to understand what her act means, before she has raised even questions of meaning for herself. She is launched into 'self'-consciousness, a self-regard of critical awkwardness and embarrassment, where the consciousness is clearly the implant of the other.

The more her spontaneous gestures and movements are inhibited, the more her sense of self will be representational and not felt to be real. She will speak before, or instead of, acting. She will not put thought between impulse and action, but will be unable to act except on, or after, thought. It is for this reason that the great educators like John Dewey and A.S. Neil made self-directed activity by the child a basic building block of mental health. 'My function has been to encourage all activity, good and bad,' said Homer Lane (1928), the Founder of the Little Commonwealth, a self-governing colony of young delinquents.

Repeated blocks to self-directed activity harden the felt dualism of experience into a rigid split. A child's social self will be visible, but her other self hidden. She may feel she needs to cultivate her private self to repel the demands and intrusions of the world. It becomes the place of secrets and lies, terms of a claim, angrily seized, to stake out an inner territory that is free from the colonizing concerns and intentions of others. In these circumstances her mind becomes a refuge within which to live, rather than one aspect of her process of engagement and interaction. She may dream but she is lonely.

We are back, in a way, to Simon's view of true and false faces. Simon's face is not always what and where he feels himself to be.

Sometimes he feels he resides deeper inside himself. When his face is a mask, his transactions with others, his 'face rituals' involve the part of himself he values the least.

But there is something else about Simon's interactions. When I make any observation of him that he can take, rightly, to reveal a personal or professional view of human aspiration and tragedy, of conflict, struggle and health, he bristles for a moment and then produces, defensively, an example of another culture where alternative philosophies and social arrangements prevail.

I am at these times deranged by fury. It is only with the greatest of effort that I am able to resist the urge to retaliate with the psychotherapist's great weapon, invented precisely for this kind of situation – the interpretation. After all, Simon's 'touchy' behaviour indicates that he is touched. I am closing in on the inner sanctum. He is firing warning shots across my bows. But I know there is more to it. I am reminded, too much, of my irritated discomfort in conversations with Robert, the boy who thought he was, or could be, a girl.

The reason that the existence of other cultures disturbs us is because it challenges the secure assumptions and comfortable sense of certainty in our way of life. It turns our own value system on its head. It pours scorn on our convictions, so deeply held, of what is natural and normal. Things could be otherwise, because they are otherwise. It is not 'obvious', for example, that children should be required by law to go to school. All communities educate, some in very different ways. It is not preordained that men go out to work, wearing trousers and thinking about football; and women, in dresses, stay at home, look after children and knit jumpers. Nor is the nuclear family the only acceptable model of people living together and raising children. There is the kibbutz and the commune.

One male missionary, over twenty-one, lying on top of a woman, always younger, behind closed bedroom doors, is not the first and final word on sexual love between human beings. We know that in other societies children witness adult nudity and parental intercourse as a matter of routine, whereas for us these experiences constitute 'traumas' which contribute to neuroses. We discourage adult nudity because of its potential for over-stimulation and the projection of envy or guilt. We believe children will misinterpret parental intercourse as an attack by the man on the woman. Elsewhere, children who have the advantage of repeated and diverse observations, soon learn that intercourse is not mortal combat, but an enjoyable, mutual transaction.

Millions of fine people, in all jobs and professions, in all walks of life, in present and past times, are and were homosexuals. We can be certain that contempt for the different practices of others is a refusal of the recognition that our own way of life is just as invented as any other.

Any suggestion of difference threatens to reveal the contingent or arbitrary nature of our own culture and evokes outrage and vicious retaliation. When Geza Roheim, the psychoanalytic theorist of culture, left Hungary in 1938, it was, according to one commentator, 'a toss-up whether he was in greater danger from the Communists or from the Fascists' (La Barre-Geza Roheim, 1966). Shot by both sides, Roheim certainly had the ability to stir things up a little.

Roheim argued that civilization can best be understood as a monumental effort on the part of growing children to protect themselves from the experience of separation anxiety, the ultimate distress that, he believed, cannot be borne. In all their cultural enterprises, men and women seek substitutes for the lost mother. These enterprises have one feature in common: 'They unite one human being to the other, they are cunning devices adopted by man, the infant, against being left alone.' The child's constant search for a substitute mother provides the civilizing process with its momentum. The paradox of civilization is that people become civilized in order to remain infants. All culture is a cleverly disguised attempt to return to the womb.

As an argument it is of course over-inclusive and reductive, and we are trained nowadays to move swiftly on from such general propositions to the minutiae of the particular. In this way we ensure that we remain pure but irrelevant, deep but meaningless. If we do not claim too much, the mistakes we make will never be big ones. The sad irony is that Roheim's analysis, far from laying bare the underlying universal structure of all human culture, seems a devastatingly accurate insight into the particular British way of life at this time. We huddle in smaller and smaller units, behind grilles and window locks, hoping for tax cuts which promise only the hope of uninterrupted personal satiety and comfort. Our political debate, conducted within a collective myth of stranger anxiety, is dominated by fearful retreat from the greedy community of others, who are felt to encroach, attack, steal or otherwise demand. Products, material and financial, are advertised with the guarantee of 'security' or 'peace of mind'. The funny thing is, the whole procedure is carried out in the name of an attack on the 'nanny' welfare state. The not-so-funny consequence is a furious return of the repressed outside the home, in road and street life of spiralling anxiety.

The novelist Tobias Wolfe begins his novel *This Boy's Life* (1989) with a quote from Oscar Wilde: 'The first duty in life is to assume a pose. Nobody has yet discovered what the second duty is' (Ellman, 1988) This boy's story ends with the announcement of the discovery of the second duty. Like many great discoveries, it has always been staring us in the face.

To say that the first identity is a social product is not to say that all identity is alienated, that no particular identity is better than any other, and that the form of social arrangements is therefore, a matter of indifference. The issue is wrongly posed, as if the individual and society are opposite terms, locked in irreconcilable contradiction.

We are all, it is understood, a collage of ourselves and others, a composite of bits of us and bits of other people. How could it be otherwise? Only, perhaps, if we were born alone, as in Gary's dream, tourist maps and phrase books in our hands, freestanding, moving and speaking, on the hillside where Oedipus was abandoned; a quick look around, then a mosey down to the local settlements to think about mixing in with the natives for a while and maybe get some breakfast. It is not like that. More importantly, why would we want it to be different from the way it is?

There is a mood that appears to draw us towards others in order not to feel alone, but there is another which is more primary – the exploration, sometimes joyful, sometimes playful, on the part of ourselves as members of a curious and social species, that takes place within a relatedness that is already the essence of our being. Such relatedness is apparent from the beginning, in all interactions between parents and infants. It continues in the excited and tense play of similarities and frictions in relationships with other people in the world including, in the internal world, their images and representations.

The child first discovers who her parents and others say she is and then shapes her identity into a performance of that role. This first act of naming from the parents is their gift of welcoming reception. She already belongs; this ceremony serves to mark formally the acknowledgement and recognition of that fact.

Other people, of course, always give us presents that *they* think we will want. The child's acceptance is her loving response of gratitude. Her slow discovery, however, is that her membership card is a statement also of restraint. The privileges it allows are predicated on the preclusion of other possibilities. To be in one club is not to be in another. If she is given a girl's name, she cannot live a boy's life. If she is the oldest, middle or youngest child, there is a route that is clearly marked out for her, with paths on either side that she must not follow.

A rough guide to how 'dutifully' accepted this pose is for her will be the extent to which she later feels compelled to harangue others to confirm, sustain or deny it. The strength of feeling that surrounds the defence of, or insistence on, her assumed identity, will probably indicate the unacknowledged resentment and rage at a set of labels she felt were too forcefully applied in her early life.

'If someone hands you something,' said the fourteen-year-old girl, 'you can say you don't want it . . . if they just leave it on you or on

> something of yours, there is nothing you can do. You have to keep it. But if someone forces you to have what you don't want, you don't have to keep it. You can do what you want with it. Can't you?'

You can. The second duty in life is to acknowledge and accept the identities we have assumed from interaction with those on whom we have depended, and then subject these poses, the faces we have made, to critical but compassionate, scrutiny. It is the paradox of change. Only by accepting who and what we are can we be something and somebody else. We know this from our work with those at the extremes of distress – the heavy drinker must admit he is an alcoholic in order not to be enslaved to alcohol; the bereaved lover must say he cannot now survive in order to be able to live again. It is not, as psychoanalytic writers have rightly stressed in their accounts of adolescence, a question merely of taking positions that are contrary to our parents. That keeps us tied up in exactly the same place, reading the same script but changing only positive statements into negative. It is more like having the courage to improvise within the script we have anyway co-written, perhaps to discover in the course of this that we are creating an entirely new play.

But it is not either a task only for adolescence. At no time is any identity worthwhile when it depends on somebody else's identity loss. Freud showed that man always buys his own adulthood not only by exercising his maturing faculties, but by selling down the river the child inside him. From her perspective, the young person knows herself to be enlivened by strong drives of sex and aggression but is frightened these may cause her to lose the support of her protective and loving carers, owing to her relentless search for pleasure and her angry and envious fantasies of destruction. She feels, then, she must fight her impulses and passions. But many of her other anxieties, and perhaps these as well, will be the worries of her trainers. To that extent her anxiety will be learned, the effect of the original vulnerability of her early life situation and social world.

As Erik Erikson (1973) said, where the consequence of this first dependence and vulnerability is the imposition of *guilt*, then childhood is the model of all oppression and enslavement, a kind of inner colonization, which later forces grown-ups to accept inner repression and self-restriction. In fact, it is probably the case that other oppressions would not be possible without this inner precursor, in which a negative identity of being somehow at fault, or not good enough, is imposed on the oppressed child or race, and with it the projection of self-hate.

As a response and solution to the oppression of youth, young leaders at a Re-evaluation Co-Counselling Workshop in England in 1990 formulated a list of demands 'by young people, for young people':

1 All young people who wish to must be allowed to vote.
2 All laws related to age must be removed
3 Young people are not the property of their parents, and the law must be changed to reflect this.
4 All sexual and physical abuse of young people must stop immediately.
5 Young people must run their own schools.
6 Young people must produce their own TV and films.
7 Every young person has the right to food, warmth, shelter and a good education.
8 Buildings with good facilities must be provided in every area, to be run by young people for young people.
9 Architecture and design must consider young people (e.g., toilets, door handles, car interiors, etc.)
10 Young people's economic situation must be improved: there must be worthwhile jobs with worthwhile pay for young workers; pocket money must be provided by the state (not left to parents to provide).
11 The importance of parents, teachers, and other allies of young people must be recognized and rewarded. Good support and pay must be provided for these important workers.
12 All mistreatment of young people by other young people must stop, and must be replaced with complete respect, so that we can unite and achieve these important goals.

The critical test of whether relationships are oppressive or not is the extent to which the parties involved understand fully the context and consequences of their actions and whether there is parity in their powers to consent and refuse. Clearly, such conditions are unlikely to pertain to present adult-child relationships, and the above series of demands by young leaders addresses itself to the process in which oppressive and exploitative inequalities might begin to be reduced or eliminated through empowerment of the young. Adult responsibilities in terms of rights and duties will also be a major factor. Here lies the problem.

For the alienated adult, children are the fiercest critics of established custom and practice, the extreme version of Simon. Their incomplete, preformed, precommitted diversity and their free-floating potential, are a threat to the self-imposed restraints, routines and compromises of the half-lived adult life of anomie, the finished product. We adults look, then, in anxious anticipation to the infant's genitals in a move that ushers in restriction alongside definition. As a 'boy' or a 'girl' the new person no longer threatens to awaken the unconfident and fluid status of our own sexual identity, revealed to us when we dream. As 'just like his father', the disturbance of infinite otherness and unpredictability is settled. As 'our' son or 'my' daughter, difference and lack are denied in the claim of ownership. There is no gap within which movement need be felt or dared. We stand close and still together.

There is another way. We can make our social world inclusive, at school, work and play, and admit that growth from youth into old age requires real opportunity and worthwhile experience for everybody. Where our culture is a better theatre for personal contribution and achievement, it does not collude with passive and vicarious living through the young, whether by idealization or abuse. It becomes also a world that is worth growing up into.

Many young people are deprived of secure position and opportunity for meaningful participation in the cultures into which they are born. They are, and feel, excluded, and are hopeless about reaching that elevated status, so confidently assumed by the specially favoured sons and daughters of the middle classes. The crisis of youth is the despair of a present that is absent without leave and a future that has forgotten to hand out invitations.

Most, said Goodman (1960), face a stark dilemma of belief. Either the adult world of work and property is a benign but pointless chicanery in which they might manage to wheel and deal and charm their way through, although probably with less material success than the more privileged. Or what they see is indeed the best of all possible worlds from which they, unfortunately, are disqualified because inept, fit only for the margins into which they are swept. Such considerations do not inspire creative commitment.

We make narrow the options of our young and permit them access to adulthood only by way of inductions or initiations – the system of compulsory schooling – that function to restrict them to circumscribed identities. We punish or threaten truants and transgressors. The fear, presumably, is that the young will overthrow the prevailing systems of power, privilege and authority. But this fear is the reverse side of the wish; we are ambivalent. The zoo that we like to visit is a sorry place. Proud, of course, of our children's performances of courtesy and good behaviour, and relieved as we are at their safe protection from the dangers of life in the wild, we are saddened, somewhere else, by their compliance and confinement. They must adapt and fit in, as we did, but must break free and rebel on our behalf. Our contradictory requirements drive them mad. They have no choice: they become adolescents.

References and further reading

Abraham, K., *Selected Papers on Psychoanalysis*. Maresfield Reprints 1979.

Adams, P.; Berg, L. Berger, N. Duane, M. Neill, A. S. Ollendorf, R., *Children's Rights*. Panther Books 1972.

Aries, P., *Centuries of Childhood*. Vintage Books 1962.

Becker, E., *The Structure of Evil*. New York: George Braziller 1968.

– *The Birth and Death of Meaning*. Penguin Education 1971.

Blos, P., *On Adolescence*. The Free Press 1962.

Bollas, C., *The Shadow of the Object: Psychoanalysis of the Unthought Known*. Free Association Books 1987.

Buckler, J., *The Adolescent Years*. Castlemead Publications 1987.

Clare, A., 'Acne Agonies – Review of Normal Adolescence'. By the Committee on Adolescence – Group for the Advancement of Psychiatry. Crosby Lockwood Staples 1974. *New Society* May 1974.

Crisp, Q., *The Naked Civil Servant*. Jonathan Cape 1968.

Dalsimer, K., *Female Adolescence*. Yale University Press 1986.

Davies, J. and Coggans, N., *The Facts About Adolescent Drug Abuse*. Cassell 1991.

Debray, R., *Revolution in the Revolution?* Pelican Books 1968.

Dennison, G., *The Lives of Children*. Vintage Books 1970.

Dockar-Drysdale, B., *The Provision of Primary Experience*. Free Association Books 1990.

– *Therapy and Consultation in Child Care*. Free Association Books 1993.

Dostoyevsky, F., *Crime and Punishment*. Penguin Classics 1970.

Dylan, B. 'Highway 61 Revisited'. Knopf 1985

Eliot, T. S., *Collected Poems, 1909–1962*. Faber and Faber 1963.

Ellman, R. *Oscar Wilde*. Penguin Books 1988.

Emerson, R. W., *Essays* (Ed. Dent, S. P.). Everyman 1906.

Ennew, J., *The Sexual Exploitation of Children*. Polity Press 1986.

Erikson, E., *Identity: Youth and Crisis*. Faber and Faber 1968.

– *In Search of Common Ground*. Norton 1973.

Falchikov, N., 'Adolescent images of adolescence'. *Journal of Adolescence* June 1989.

Ferenczi, S., *Thalassa*. Marefield Library 1989.

Firestone, S., *The Dialectic of Sex*. Jonathan Cape 1971.

Freud, A., 'Adolescence', *The Psychoanalytic Study of the Child* 1958.

Freud, S., *Totem and Taboo*. Standard Edition, Vol. 13, Hogarth Press 1913.

Gibran, K., *The Prophet*. Heinemann 1965.

Greenberg, H., 'The Widening Gyre: Transformations of the Omnipotent Quest During Adolescence', in *International Review of Psychoanalysis* 1975.

Greenberg, J. and Mitchell, S., *Object Relations in Psychoanalytic Theory*. Harvard University Press 1983.

Goodman, P., *Five Years – Thoughts During a Useless Time*. Vintage Books 1969.

– *Growing Up Absurd*. Vintage Books 1960.

– *Little Prayers and Finite Experience*. Wildwood House 1973.

Hadfield, J. A., *Childhood and Adolescence*. Penguin Books 1962.

Harris, M., *Collected Papers of Martha Harris and Esther Bick*. Clunie Press 1987.

Hollingworth, L., *The Psychology of the Adolescent*. Partridge 1929.
Ibsen, H., *An Enemy of the People*. N. Herne Books 1989.
Illich, I., *Limits to Medicine*. Pelican Books 1977.
Inhelder, B. and Piaget, J., *The Growth of Logical Thinking from Childhood to Adolescence*. Basic Books 1958.
Isaacs, S., *Intellectual Growth in Young Children*. Routledge 1930.
– *Social Development in Young Children*. Routledge 1933.
James, C., Atkin, P., *The Wall of Death*. Warner Brothers Music 1974.
Kincaid, J., *Child Loving*. Routledge 1992.
Kovel, J., *The Age of Desire*. Pantheon Books 1981.
Kureishi, H., *The Buddha of Suburbia*. Faber and Faber 1990.
La Barre, W., Geza Roheim in *Psychoanalytic Pioneers*. Ed. Alexander, Eisenstein and Grotjahn. Basic Books 1966.
Lacan, J. *Ecrits*. Senil 1966.
Lane, H., *Talks to Parents and Teachers*. Allen and Unwin 1928.
Larkin, P., *High Windows*. Faber and Faber 1974.
Levi-Strauss, C. *The Elementary Structures of Kinship*. Eyre and Spottiswood 1969.
Lowen, A., *Fear of Life*. Collier Books 1981.
Mahler, M., Pine, F., and Bergman, A., *The Psychological Birth of the Human Infant: Separation and Individuation*. Basic Books 1975.
Mannoni, M., *The Child, His Illness and the Others*. Penguin Books 1973.
Meltzer, D., *Sexual States of Mind*. Clunie Press 1967.
O'Brown, N., *Life Against Death*. Routledge and Kegan Paul 1959.
Orton, J., *Loot*. Methuen 1967.
Perls, F., Hefferline, R., Goodman, P., *Gestalt Therapy*. Souvenir Press 1972.
Phillips, A., *Winnicott*. Fontana Press 1988.
– *On Kissing, Tickling and Being Bored*. Faber and Faber 1993.
– *On Flirtation*. Faber and Faber 1994.
Raymond, J., *The Transsexual Empire*. The Women's Press 1980.
Rycroft, C., *A Critical Dictionary of Psychoanalysis*. Penguin Books 1972.
Salinger, J. D., *The Catcher in the Rye*. Penguin Books 1958.
Shepher, J., 'Mate selection among second generation kibbutz adolescents and adults: incest avoidance and negative imprinting'. *Archives of Sexual Behaviour* 1:293–307 1971.
Spiro, M. E., *Children of the Kibbutz*. Harvard University Press 1958.
Stern, D., *The Interpersonal World of the Infant: A View from Psychoanalysis and Developmental Psychology*. Basic Books 1985.
Stone, L., *The Family: Sex and Marriage in England 1500–1800*. Weidenfeld & Nicolson 1977.
Stullivan, H. S., *Clinical Studies in Psychiatry*. Norton 1973.
de Vries, P., *Tunnel of Love*. Viking Press 1954.
Welsh, I., *Trainspotting*. Minerva 1994.
Wilde, O., *The Picture of Dorian Gray*. Penguin Books 1949.
Wilde, O., *Prose Writings and Poems*. Everyman 1996.
Wilson, P., and Bottomley, V., *The Emotional Climate in the Classroom*. University of Cardiff monograph 1978.
Winnicott, D. W., *Playing and Reality*. Penguin Books 1974.
– *Through Paediatrics to Psychoanalysis*. Tavistock 1958.
– *The Maturational Processes and the Facilitating Environment*. Hogarth Press 1965.
Wolfe, Tobias, *This Boy's Life*. Picador 1989.

Index